W9-CUI-464

Careers in Focus

Education

Ferguson Publishing Company
Chicago, Illinois

Andrew Morkes, *Managing Editor-Career Publications*
Carol Yehling, *Senior Editor*
Anne Paterson, *Editor*
Nora Walsh, *Assistant Editor*

Copyright © 2002 Ferguson Publishing Company

Library of Congress Cataloging-in-Publication Data

Careers in focus. Education.
    p. cm.
Includes index.
  ISBN 0-89434-401-3
  1. School employees--Vocational guidance--United States. 2.
Teachers--Vocational guidance--United States. I. Title: Education. II.
Ferguson Publishing Company. III. Title.
  LB2831.58 .C35 2001
  370'.23'73--dc21
                                        2001002894

Printed in the United States of America

Cover photo courtesy Jose L. Pelaez/The Stock Market

Published and distributed by
Ferguson Publishing Company
200 West Jackson Boulevard, 7th Floor
Chicago, Illinois 60606
800-306-9941
www.fergpubco.com

All rights reserved. No part of this publication may be reproduced, stored in
a retrieval system, or transmitted by any means, electronic, mechanical, photocopying or otherwise, without the prior permission of the publisher.

Table of Contents

Introduction

The majority of people involved in education are engaged in teaching. Teaching responsibilities can vary greatly from job to job in terms of subjects, schedules, and assigned duties. For example, elementary school teachers typically work with one group of children all day, while secondary school teachers (junior and senior high school) meet four, five, or more groups of students throughout the day. College professors may only present a few lectures a day, but must also conduct scholarly research.

Teachers of younger children perform many of the roles of a parent, so the jobs of the preschool, kindergarten, and elementary school teachers include the personal and social responsibilities that are assumed by parents at home. These jobs, of course, also include the full gamut of responsibilities for the emotional and intellectual growth of children. Responsibilities of teachers of grades K-6 include teaching, selecting and planning coursework, grading homework, and evaluating student achievement. They also participate in conferences with parents, other teachers, and administrators on problems with curriculum, instruction, and guidance.

High school teachers have basic responsibilities similar to those of elementary school teachers, but they act less as parent substitutes and are more concerned with academics. Typically, high school teachers specialize in one or two subjects. But even at the high school level, teachers will be concerned about more than the students' academic progress. They also help students deal with personal problems and advise them in matters concerning their future, such as selecting colleges and careers.

Similar to the high school teacher, the college professor shares the commitment to a specific field of knowledge, but such commitment is more intense. College professors are expected to participate in the activities of a professional society or association. Increasingly, professors are sought out as consultants in business, government, and public service.

With more demands on their time extending outside of the classroom, college teachers may find difficulty in spending as much time with students as they would like. Professors with years of experience and a high level of specialization may choose to teach at the graduate level. These teachers spend more time in research activities and work with a small number of graduate students.

At all levels of the profession, teachers today are generally better educated than they were a few years ago. All states require the minimum of a bachelor's degree for a beginning position, and many teachers have graduate degrees.

A variety of new opportunities for educators have evolved in nontraditional areas. Qualified education professionals are needed to work in agencies such as adult education programs, recreation departments, drug and alcohol abuse programs, Planned Parenthood units, and government organizations, such as the Peace Corps and Job Corps. Careers in education extend beyond the typical classroom setting.

Thousands of people are employed by professional organizations, private agencies with educational programs, and government offices of education. Every state in the United States has an office of education, which hires professionals to monitor and make recommendations for local school policies. The federal government also employs professionals to ensure that legislative mandates regarding education are carried out at the state and local levels. Federal education officials are concerned with such areas as bilingual education, transportation, and school health.

Colleges and universities hire workers with an education background to work as administrators. These workers handle financial aid distribution, record keeping, course development, and hiring.

Most positions in education outside the classroom require teaching experience. For example, school and college administrators, including superintendents and principals, often first serve as teachers. Association leaders and educators in government offices also often begin their careers as teachers. To be qualified and experienced for these higher-level positions, most education administrators and government officials have also completed graduate study in education.

Many educational publishing houses prefer to hire textbook editors with teaching experience. As former teachers, these editors are not only experts in the subject matter, but are also better able to determine whether the material is appropriate for the age and level a book is intended for, and whether instructions are clear and easy for a teacher to use.

Most teachers belong to a professional union such as the National Education Association or the American Federation of Teachers. These professional organizations grew steadily after World War II. Most teachers also join other associations or societies that represent their own subject areas or fields of specialization.

Improvements pushed for and attained by professional organizations include reduced teaching loads to allow more time for planning and evaluating, and budgetary allowances that permit teachers to attend professional meetings. Other policy changes benefiting teachers include laws guaranteeing due process, establishing grievance procedures, ensuring fair dismissal procedures, and protecting teachers' rights and academic freedom.

A job description for teaching is easy to provide. More difficult is the task of conveying the essence of teaching—how it feels to be a teacher. People interested in learning more about the life of a teacher may want to read Tracy Kidder's book, *Among Schoolchildren*. This book closely follows one year in the life of a fifth-grade teacher and her class in a depressed section of Holyoke, Massachusetts.

Teachers must be extremely dedicated to their students, to the subject(s) they teach, and to the notion of education in general. Perhaps it is for this reason that teaching is frequently referred to as a "calling" rather than a career.

According to the U.S. Department of Labor, employment in the field of education is expected to increase by 15 percent between 1998 and 2008, the same growth rate projected for all industries combined. Aside from growth within the field, many job openings will arise from the need to replace workers who retire or change occupations.

The fastest growing careers in the education industry include secondary school teachers, college and university professors and administrators, and counselors. The employment of adult education teachers, elementary school teachers, and preschool and kindergarten teachers is expected to grow at an average rate. In addition, the enrollment of foreign and special education students has been growing rapidly in recent years, spurring demand for specialized educators such as ESL and special education teachers.

Anticipated growth in this industry is due, for the most part, to two major trends. First, the number of school-aged children is expected to grow in the next decade. At the same time, the federal government has become committed to lowering the number of students per class to improve educational environments, increasing the need for more teachers.

Though college enrollment is also expected to increase, competition for full-time faculty and administrator positions will remain high. Lower paid, part-time instructors, such as visiting professors and graduate students, are replacing tenure-track faculty positions. Organizations such as the American Association of University Professors and the American Federation of Teachers are working to prevent the loss of full-time jobs, as well as help part-time instructors receive better pay and benefits.

More instructors will find work in community colleges and other adult education programs. The federal government is committed to providing vocational training for high school graduates who choose not to enroll immediately in four-year colleges or universities. These "school-to-work" programs that prepare graduating seniors for high-wage technical jobs will require trained adult and vocational education teachers.

Each article in this book discusses a particular education occupation in detail. The articles in *Careers in Focus: Education* appear in Ferguson's *Encyclopedia of Careers and Vocational Guidance*, but have been updated and revised with the latest information from the U.S. Department of Labor and other sources. The **Overview** section is a brief introductory description of the duties and responsibilities of someone in the career. Oftentimes, a career may have a variety of job titles. When this is the case, alternative career titles are presented in this section. The **History** section describes the history of the particular job as it relates to the overall development of its industry or field. **The Job** describes the primary and secondary duties of the job. **Requirements** discusses high school and postsecondary education and training requirements, any certification or licensing necessary, and any other personal requirements for success in the job. **Exploring** offers suggestions on how to gain some experience in or knowledge of the particular job before making a firm educational and financial commitment. The focus is on what can be done while still in high school (or in the early years of college) to gain a better understanding of the job. The **Employers** section gives an overview of typical places of employment for the job. **Starting Out** discusses the best ways to land that first job, be it through the college placement office, newspaper ads, or personal contact. The **Advancement** section describes what kind of career path to expect from the job and how to get there. **Earnings** lists salary ranges and describes the typical fringe benefits. The **Work Environment** section describes the typical surroundings and conditions of employment, whether indoors or outdoors, noisy or quiet, social or independent, and so on. Also discussed are typical hours worked, any seasonal fluctuations, and the stresses and strains of the job. The **Outlook** section summarizes the job in terms of the general economy and industry projections. For the most part, Outlook information is obtained from the Bureau of Labor Statistics and is supplemented by information taken from professional associations. Job growth terms follow those used in the *Occupational Outlook Handbook:* Growth described as "much faster than the average" means an increase of 36 percent or more. Growth described as "faster than the average" means an increase of 21 to 35 percent. Growth described as "about as fast as the average" means an increase of 10 to 20 percent. Growth described as "little change or more slowly than the average" means an increase of 0 to 9 percent. "Decline" means a decrease of 1 percent or more. Each article ends with **For More Information,** which lists organizations that can provide career information on training, education, internships, scholarships, and job placement.

Adult and Vocational Education Teachers

School Subjects
English
Psychology

Personal Skills
Communication/ideas
Helping/teaching

Work Environment
Primarily indoors
Primarily one location

Minimum Education Level
Bachelor's degree

Salary Range
$13,080 to $34,430 to $47,430+

Certification or Licensing
Required by certain states

Outlook
As fast as the average

Overview

Adult and vocational education teachers teach basic academic subjects to adults who did not finish high school or who are new to speaking English. They help prepare post-high school students and other adults for specific occupations and provide personal enrichment. Adult education teachers offer basic education courses, such as reading and writing, or continuing education courses, such as literature and music. Vocational education teachers offer courses designed to prepare adults for specific occupations, such as data processor or automobile mechanic. There are approximately 588,000 adult and vocational education teachers employed in the United States.

History

In American colonial times, organized adult education was started to help people make up for schooling missed as children or to help people prepare for jobs. Apprenticeships were an early form of vocational education in the American colonies as individuals were taught a craft by working with a skilled person in a particular field. For example, a young boy might agree to work for a printer for five to ten years and at the end of that time be able to open up his own printing business. Training programs continued to develop as carpenters, bricklayers, and other craftspeople learned their skills through vocational training courses. Peak periods in adult education typically occurred during times of large-scale immigration. Evening schools filled with foreign-born persons eager to learn the language and culture of their new home and to prepare for the tests necessary for citizenship.

In 1911, Wisconsin established the first State Board of Vocational and Adult Education in the country, and in 1917 the federal government supported the continuing education movement by funding vocational training in public schools for individuals over the age of 14. Immediately after World War II, the federal government took another large stride in financial support of adult and vocational education by creating the G.I. Bill of Rights, which provided money for veterans to pursue further job training.

Today colleges and universities, vocational high schools, private trade schools, private businesses, and other organizations offer adults the opportunity to prepare for a specific occupation or pursue personal enrichment. More than 20 million people in the United States take advantage of this opportunity each year, creating many jobs for teachers in this field.

The Job

Adult and vocational education courses take place in a variety of settings, such as high schools, universities, religious institutions, and businesses. The responsibilities of an adult or vocational education teacher are similar to those of a school teacher and include planning and conducting lectures, supervising the use of equipment, grading homework, evaluating students, writing and preparing reports, and counseling students.

Adult education is divided into two main areas: basic education and continuing education. Basic education includes reading, writing, and mathematics courses and is designed for adult students who have not finished high school. Many of these students are taking basic education courses to earn the equivalent of a high school diploma (the General Equivalency

Diploma, or GED). Some high school graduates who received poor grades in high school also enroll in basic education classes before attending a four-year college. Recent immigrants may take basic education classes to learn to read, write, and do arithmetic in the language of their new country.

Unlike basic education, continuing education for adults is aimed at students who have finished high school or college and are taking courses for personal enrichment. Class topics might include creative writing, art appreciation, photography, history, and a host of other subjects. Often businesses will enroll employees in continuing education courses as part of job training to help them develop computer skills, learn to write grant proposals, or become convincing public speakers. Sometimes, businesses will hire an adult education teacher to come into the business to train employees on-site. These *continuing education teachers* are called *training representatives.*

Vocational education teachers prepare students for specific careers that do not require college degrees, such as cosmetologist, chef, or welder. They demonstrate techniques and then advise the students as they attempt these techniques. They also lecture on the class subject, and direct discussion groups. Instruction by a vocational education teacher may lead to the student's certification, so teachers may follow a specific course plan approved by an accrediting association. They may also be involved in directing a student to an internship, and to local job opportunities.

Whether teaching in a basic education or continuing education classroom, adult and vocational education teachers work with small groups of students. In addition to giving lectures, they assign text books and homework assignments. They prepare and administer exams, and grade essays and presentations. Adult and vocational education teachers also meet with students individually to discuss class progress and grades. Some courses are conducted as part of a long-distance education program (traditionally known as correspondence courses). For a distance education course, teachers prepare course materials, assignments, and work schedules to be sent to students, and then grade the work when it is turned in by the students.

Requirements

High School

An adult education teacher will generally focus on a particular area of study, so take the high school courses that best suit your interests. You'll also need to follow a college preparatory plan, taking courses in English, math, foreign language, history, and government. Speech and communications courses will help you prepare for speaking in front of groups of people. Writing skills are very important, no matter what subject you teach, because you'll be preparing reports, lesson plans, and grading essays.

Postsecondary Training

Before becoming an adult education teacher, you'll need to gain some professional experience in your area of teaching. A bachelor's degree is also usually required. Requirements vary according to the subject and level being taught, the organization or institution offering the course, and the state in which the instruction takes place. Specific skills, however, are often enough to secure a continuing education teaching position. For example, a person well-trained in painting, with some professional success in the area, may be able to teach a course on painting even without a college degree or teaching certificate.

Certification or Licensing

There is no national certifying board for adult education teachers, but some states require their own teaching certification. Most community and junior colleges, however, require only a bachelor's degree of their teachers. Teachers in vocational education programs may have to be certified in their profession. If teaching English as a second language (ESL), you'll probably have to take some required workshops and seminars. For information on certification, students should contact local adult education programs and the department of education in the state in which they are interested in teaching.

Other Requirements

As a teacher, you should be able to deal with students at different skill levels, including some who might not have learned proper study habits or who have a different first language. This requires patience, as well as the ability to track the progress of each individual student. Good communication skills are essential, as you'll need to explain things clearly and to answer questions completely.

Exploring

Adult education classes are often held at high schools; if this is the case at your school, take the opportunity to discuss career questions with teachers before or after a class. You may also get the opportunity to observe one of these classes. Some of your high school teachers may be teaching adult or vocational education courses in the evenings; talk to them about the difference between teaching high school and teaching in an adult education program. Registering for a continuing education or vocational education course is another way of discovering the skills and disciplines needed to succeed in this field; if you have an interest in a particular subject not taught at your school, seek out classes at community colleges.

Your school may have a peer tutoring program which would introduce you to the requirements of teaching. You could also volunteer to assist in special educational activities at a nursing home, church, or community center.

Employers

Adult education teachers can find work in a variety of different schools and education programs. Community and junior colleges regularly have openings for teachers. Specially trained teachers can work for state-funded programs, such as literacy and ESL programs. Teachers are also hired for long-distance education programs, and to lead continuing education courses for corporations and professional associations. Teachers are often needed in such institutions as prisons, hospitals, retirement communities, and group homes for disabled adults.

Starting Out

Most people entering the field have some professional experience in a particular area, a desire to share that knowledge with other adults, and a teaching certificate or academic degree. When pursuing work as an adult education teacher, you should contact colleges, private trade schools, vocational high schools, or other appropriate institutions to receive additional information about employment opportunities. Many colleges, technical schools, and state departments of education offer job lines or bulletin boards of job listings. You can also often find job openings in the classifieds of local newspapers.

Advancement

A skilled adult or vocational education teacher may become a full-time teacher, school administrator, or director of a vocational guidance program. To be an administrator, a master's degree or a doctorate may be required. Advancement also may take the form of higher pay and additional teaching assignments. For example, a person may get a reputation as a skilled ceramics teacher and be hired by other adult education organizations as an instructor.

Earnings

Earnings vary widely according to the subject, the number of courses taught, the teacher's experience, and the geographic region where the institution is located. Full-time vocational education teachers earned an average salary of $34,430 a year, according to the U.S. Department of Labor. The majority of full-time instructors averaged between $24,890 and $45,230 a year, with some highly skilled and experienced teachers earning even more. Adult education teachers averaged $24,800 in 1998. The lowest 10 percent earned less than $13,080, and the highest 10 percent earned more than $47,430 annually.

Because many adult and vocational education teachers are employed part-time, they are often paid by the hour or by the course, with no health insurance or other benefits. Hourly rates range from $6 to $50.

Work Environment

Working conditions vary according to the type of class being taught and the number of students participating. Courses are usually taught in a classroom setting but may also be in a technical shop, laboratory, art studio, music room, or other location depending on the subject matter. Of course, when teaching in such settings as prisons or hospitals, adult education teachers must travel to the students as opposed to the students traveling to the teacher's classroom. Average class size is usually between 10 and 30 students, but may vary, ranging from one-on-one instruction to large lectures attended by 60 or more students.

Some adult and vocational education teachers may only work nine or ten months a year, with summers off. About half of the adult and vocational education teachers work part-time, averaging anywhere from two to 20 hours of work per week. For those employed full-time, the average workweek is between 35 and 40 hours. Much of the work is in the evening or on weekends, as many adult students work on weekdays.

Outlook

Employment opportunities in the field of adult education are expected to grow as fast as the average through 2008. Adults recognize the importance of further education and training for succeeding in today's workplace. In fact, many courses are subsidized by companies that want their employees trained in the latest skills and technology of their field. The biggest growth areas are projected to be in computer technology, automotive mechanics, and medical technology. As demand for adult and vocational education teachers continues to grow, major employers will be vocational high schools, private trade schools, community colleges, and private adult education enterprises.

Many "school-to-work" programs have evolved across the country as a result of the School-to-Work Opportunities Act of 1994. To prepare more graduating seniors for the high-wage jobs, "tech prep" programs offer course work in both academic and vocational subject matter. As more of these programs are developed, vocational education teachers will find many more opportunities to work in high schools and training schools.

For More Information

For information about conferences and publications, contact:

American Association for Adult and Continuing Education
1200 19th Street, NW, Suite 300
Washington, DC 20036
Tel: 202-429-5131
Email: aaace10@aol.com
Web: http://www.cdlr.tamu.edu/tcall/aaace/

For information about publications, current legislation, and school-to-work programs, contact:

Association for Career and Technical Education
1410 King Street
Alexandria, VA 22314
Tel: 800-826-9972
Email: acte@acteonline.org
Web: http://www.acteonline.org

For information about government programs, contact:

U.S. Department of Education
400 Maryland Avenue, SW
Washington, DC 20202-0498
Tel: 800-872-5327
Email: customerservice@inet.ed.gov
Web: http://www.ed.gov

Career and Employment Counselors and Technicians

School Subjects	
Business	
Psychology	
Sociology	

School Subjects
Business
Psychology
Sociology

Personal Skills
Communication/ideas
Helping/teaching

Work Environment
Primarily indoors
Primarily one location

Minimum Education Level
High school diploma

Salary Range
$15,000 to $38,650 to $100,000+

Certification or Licensing
Voluntary

Outlook
Faster than the average

Overview

Career and employment counselors and technicians, who are also known as *vocational counselors,* provide advice to individuals or groups about occupations, careers, career decision making, career planning, and other career development-related questions or conflicts. *Career guidance technicians* collect pertinent information to support both the counselor and applicant during the job search.

History

The first funded employment office in the United States was established in San Francisco in 1886. However, it wasn't until the turn of the century that public interest in improving educational conditions began to develop. The Civic Service House in Boston began the United States' first program of vocational guidance, and the Vocational Bureau was established in 1908 to help young people choose, train, and enter appropriate careers.

The idea of vocational counseling became so appealing that by 1910 a national conference on vocational guidance was held in Boston. The federal government gave support to vocational counseling by initiating a program to assist veterans of World War I in readjusting to civilian life. During the Depression years, agencies such as the Civilian Conservation Corps and the National Youth Administration made attempts at vocational counseling.

On June 6, 1933, the Wagner-Pyser Act established the United States Employment Service. States came into the Service one by one, with each state developing its own plan under the prescribed limits of the Act. By the end of World War II, the Veterans Administration was counseling more than 50,000 veterans each month. Other state and federal government agencies now involved with vocational guidance services include the Bureau of Indian Affairs, the Bureau of Apprenticeship and Training, the Office of Manpower Development, and the Department of Education. In 1980, the National Career Development Association (NCDA), founded in 1913, established a committee for the pre-service and in-service training of vocational guidance personnel. The NCDA established a national credentialing process in 1984.

The profession of employment counseling has become important to the welfare of society as well as to the individuals within it. Each year thousands of people need help in acquiring the kinds of information that make it possible for them to take advantage of today's career opportunities.

The Job

Certified career counselors help people make decisions and plan life and career directions. They tailor strategies and techniques to the specific needs of the person seeking help. Counselors conduct individual and group counseling sessions to help identify life and career goals. They administer and interpret tests and inventories to assess abilities and interests and identify career options. They may use career planning and occupational information to help individuals better understand the work world. They assist in developing individualized career plans, teach job-hunting strategies and skills, and help develop resumes. Sometimes this involves resolving personal conflicts on the job. They also provide support for people experiencing job stress, job loss, and career transition.

Vocational-rehabilitation counselors work with disabled individuals to help the counselees understand what skills they have to offer to an employer. A good counselor knows the working world and how to obtain detailed information about specific jobs. To assist with career decisions, counselors must know about the availability of jobs, the probable future of certain jobs, the education or training necessary to enter them, the kinds of salary or other benefits that certain jobs offer, the conditions that certain jobs impose on employees (night work, travel, work outdoors), and the satisfaction that certain jobs provide their employees. *Professional career counselors* work in both private and public settings and are certified by the National Board for Certified Counselors.

College career planning and placement counselors work exclusively with the students of their universities or colleges. They may specialize in some specific area appropriate to the students and graduates of the school, such as law and education, as well as in part-time and summer work, internships, and field placements. In a liberal arts college, the students may need more assistance in identifying an appropriate career. To do this, the counselor administers interest and aptitude tests and interviews students to determine their career goals.

The counselor may work with currently enrolled students who are seeking internships and other work programs while still at school. Alumni who wish to make a career change also seek the services of the career counseling and placement office at their former schools.

College placement counselors also gather complete job information from prospective employers, and make the information available to interested students and alumni. Just as counselors try to find applicants for particular job listings, they also must seek out jobs for specific applicants. To do this, they will call potential employers to encourage them to consider a qualified individual.

College and career planning and placement counselors are responsible for the arrangements and details of on-campus interviews by large corporations and maintain an up-to-date library of vocational guidance material and recruitment literature.

Counselors also give assistance in preparing the actual job search by helping the applicant to write resumes and letters of application, as well as by practicing interview skills through role playing and other techniques. They also provide information on business procedures and personnel requirements in the applicant's chosen field. At universities with access to the

Internet, counselors will set up online accounts for students, giving them access to information regarding potential employers.

Some career planning and placement counselors work with secondary school authorities, advising them on the needs of local industries and specific preparation requirements for both employment and further education. In two-year colleges the counselor may participate in the planning of course content, and in some smaller schools the counselor may be required to teach as well.

The principal duty of career guidance technicians is to help order, catalog, and file materials relating to job opportunities, careers, technical schools, scholarships, careers in the armed forces, and other programs. Guidance technicians also help students and teachers find materials relating to a student's interests and aptitudes. These various materials may be in the form of books, pamphlets, magazine articles, microfiche, videos, computer software, or other media.

Often, career guidance technicians help students take and score self-administered tests that determine their aptitude and interest in different careers or job-related activities. If the career guidance center has audiovisual equipment, such as VCRs or film or slide projectors, career guidance technicians are usually responsible for the equipment.

Requirements

High School

In order to work in the career and employment counseling field, you must have at least a high school diploma. For most jobs in the field, however, higher education is required. In high school, in addition to studying a core curriculum, with courses in English, history, mathematics, and so on, you should take courses in psychology, sociology, and business.

Postsecondary Training

When hiring a career guidance technician, most employers look for applicants who have completed two years of training beyond high school, usually at a junior, community, or technical college. These two-year programs, which usually lead to an associate's degree, may combine classroom instruction with practical or sometimes even on-the-job experience.

In some states the minimum educational program in career and vocational counseling is a graduate degree in counseling or a related field from a regionally accredited higher education institution, and a completed supervised counseling experience, which includes career counseling. A growing number of institutions offer post-master's degrees with training in career development and career counseling. Such programs are highly recommended for people who wish to specialize in vocational and career counseling. These programs are frequently called Advanced Graduate Specialist programs or Certificates of Advanced Study programs.

For a career as a college career planning and placement counselor, the minimum educational requirement is commonly a master's degree in guidance and counseling, education, college student personnel work, behavioral science, or a related field. Graduate work includes courses in vocational and aptitude testing, counseling techniques, personnel management and occupational research, industrial relations, and group dynamics and organizational behavior.

As in any profession, there is usually an initial period of training for newly hired counselors and counselor trainees. Some of the skills needed by employment counselors, such as testing-procedures skills and interviewing skills, can only be acquired through on-the-job training.

Certification or Licensing

The National Board for Certified Counselors offers the National Certified Counselor (NCC) designation. Applicants must have earned a master's degree with a major study in counseling and take and pass the National Counselor Examination (NCE). National Certified Counselors are certified for a period of five years. In order to be recertified, NCCs must complete 100 contact clock hours of continuing education or take and pass again the NCE.

Other Requirements

A career counselor must have a good background in education, training, employment trends, the current labor market, and career resources. Counselors should be able to provide their clients with information about job tasks, functions, salaries, requirements, and the future outlook of broad occupational fields.

Knowledge of testing techniques and measures of aptitude, achievement, interests, values, and personality is required. The ability to evaluate job performance and individual effectiveness is helpful. The career counselor must also have management and administrative skills.

Exploring

Summer work in an employment agency is a good way to explore the field of employment counseling. Interviewing the director of a public or private agency might give you a better understanding of what the work involves and the qualifications such an organization requires of its counselors.

Interested high school students who enjoy working with others will find helpful experiences in working in the dean's or counselor's office. Many schools offer opportunities in peer tutoring, both in academics and in career guidance-related duties. (If your school does not have such a program in place, consider putting together a proposal to institute one. Your guidance counselor should be able to help you with this.) A student's own experience in seeking summer and part-time work is also valuable in learning what the job seeker must confront in business or industry. You could write a feature story for your school newspaper on your and others' experiences in the working world.

If you are interested in becoming a career counselor, you should seek out professional career counselors and discuss the field with them. Most people are happy to talk about what they do.

High school students interested in becoming career guidance technicians should consider working part-time or as a volunteer in a library. Such work can provide students with some of the basic skills for learning about information resources, cataloging, and filing. In addition, assisting schools or clubs with any media presentations, such as video or slide shows, will help familiarize a student with the equipment used by counselors.

Employers

Career and employment counselors work in guidance offices of high schools, colleges, and universities. They are also employed by state, federal, and other bureaus of employment, and by social service agencies.

Starting Out

Journals specializing in information for career counselors frequently have job listings or information on job hotlines and services. School placement centers also are a good source of information, both because of their standard practice of listing job openings from participating firms and because schools are a likely source of jobs for career counselors. Placement officers will be aware of which schools are looking for applicants.

To enter the field of college career planning and placement, interested alumni may consider working for their alma maters as assistants in the college or university placement office. Other occupational areas that provide an excellent background for college placement work include teaching, business, public relations, previous placement training, positions in employment agencies, and experience in psychological counseling.

Career guidance technicians should receive some form of career placement from schools offering training in that area. Newspapers may list entry-level jobs. One of the best methods, however, is to contact libraries and education centers directly to inquire about their needs for assistance in developing or staffing their career guidance centers.

Advancement

Employment counselors in federal or state employment services or in other vocational counseling agencies are usually considered trainees for the first six months of their employment. During this time, they learn the specific skills that will be expected of them during their careers with these agencies. The first year of a new counselor's employment is probationary.

Positions of further responsibility include supervisory or administrative work, which may be attained by counselors after several years of experience on the job. Advancement to administrative positions often means giving up the actual counseling work, which is not an advantage to those who enjoy working with people in need of counseling.

Opportunity for advancement for college counselors, to assistant and associate placement director, director of student personnel services, or similar administrative positions, depends largely upon the type of college or university and the size of the staff. In general, a doctorate is preferred and may be necessary for advancement.

New employees in agencies are frequently considered trainees for the first six months to a year of their employment. During the training period, they acquire the specific skills that will be required of them during their tenure with the agency. Frequently, the first year of employment is probationary. After several years' experience on the job, counselors may reach supervisory or administrative positions.

Earnings

Salaries vary greatly within the career and vocational counseling field. Median salaries for full-time educational and vocational counselors were $38,650 in 1998, according to the U.S. Department of Labor. The lowest 10 percent earned less than $21,230 and the highest 10 percent earned more than $73,920. Those in business or industry earn somewhat higher salaries.

In private practice, the range is even wider. Some practitioners earn as little as $20,000 per year and others earn in excess of $100,000 per year.

Annual earnings of career planning and placement counselors vary greatly among educational institutions, with larger institutions offering the highest salaries. Benefits include holidays and vacations, pension and retirement plans, and, in some institutions, reduced tuition.

Salaries for career guidance technicians vary according to education and experience and the geographic location of the job. In general, career guidance technicians who are graduates of two-year post-high school training programs can expect to receive starting salaries averaging $15,000 to $20,000 a year.

Work Environment

Employment counselors usually work about 40 hours a week, but some agencies are more flexible. Counseling is done in offices designed to be free from noise and distractions, to allow confidential discussions with clients.

College career planning and placement counselors also normally work a 40-hour week, although irregular hours and overtime are frequently required during the peak recruiting period. They generally work on a 12-month basis.

Career guidance technicians work in very pleasant surroundings, usually in the career guidance office of a college or vocational school. They will interact with a great number of students, some of whom are eagerly looking for work, others who are more tense and anxious. The technician must remain unruffled in order to ease any tension and provide a quiet atmosphere.

Outlook

There should be good growth in the field of employment counseling through 2008, according to the U.S. Department of Labor. Although only moderate opportunities are anticipated for employment and rehabilitation counselors in state and local governments, rapid growth is expected in the development of human resource and employment assistance programs in private business and industry, which should produce more jobs.

Libraries and schools have had increasingly limited budgets for staff and resources. Competition for jobs for career guidance technicians is increasingly stiff. The needs of outplacement centers, employment agencies, and armed forces offices are remaining somewhat stagnant. If there is an increased focus on retraining workers or educating students about career options, there may be an increase in the future demand for career guidance technicians.

For More Information

For a variety of career resources for career seekers and career counseling professionals, contact:

American Counseling Association
5999 Stevenson Avenue
Alexandria, VA 22304-3300
Tel: 800-347-6647
Web: http://www.counseling.org/

Career Planning and Adult Development Network
PO Box 1484
Pacifica, CA 94044
650-359-6911
Web: http://www.careernetwork.org/

To read the online version of Job Choices, *which provides resume and interview tips, general career information, and advice from the experts, check out NACE's Web site:*

National Association of Colleges and Employers (NACE)
62 Highland Avenue
Bethlehem, PA 18017-9085
Tel: 800-544-5272
Web: http://www.jobweb.org/

For information on certification, contact:

National Board for Certified Counselors
3 Terrace Way, Suite D
Greensboro, NC 27403-3660
Tel: 336-547-0607
Email: nbcc@nbcc.org
Web: http://www.nbcc.org/

For more information on career counselors, contact:

National Career Development Association
10820 East 45th Street, Suite 210
Tulsa, OK 74146
918-663-7060
Web: http://ncda.org

College Administrators

Business English	School Subjects
Helping/teaching Leadership/management	Personal Skills
Primarily indoors Primarily one location	Work Environment
Bachelor's degree	Minimum Education Level
$20,000 to $45,000 to $200,000+	Salary Range
None available	Certification or Licensing
Little change or more slowly than the average	Outlook

Overview

College administrators coordinate and oversee programs such as admissions and financial aid in public and private colleges and universities. They frequently work with teams of people to develop and manage student services. Administrators also oversee specific academic divisions of colleges and universities.

History

Before the Civil War, most U.S. colleges and universities managed their administration with a president, a treasurer, and a part-time librarian. Members of the faculty often were responsible for the administrative tasks of the day, and there was no uniformity in college admissions requirements.

By 1860 the average number of administrative officers in U.S. colleges was still only four, but as the job of running an institution expanded in scope and function, in response to ever-increasing student enrollment, the responsibilities of administration began to splinter. After creating positions for registrar, secretary of faculty, chief business officer, and a number of departmental deans, most schools next hired a director of admissions to oversee the application and acceptance of students. In addition, several eastern schools and a few prominent college presidents, Charles Eliot of Harvard and Nicholas Butler of Columbia among them, saw the need to establish organizations whose purpose would be to put an end to the chaos. The College Entrance Examination Board was formed to create standardized college entrance requirements. By 1910, there were 25 leading eastern colleges using the Board's exams. Today, most colleges require that a student submit standardized test scores, such as the SAT or ACT, when applying.

After World War II, returning veterans entered America's colleges and universities by the thousands. With this great influx of students, college administrators were needed to better organize the university system. During this time, financial aid administration also became a major program. Today, as the costs of a college education continue to rise dramatically, college financial aid administrators are needed to help students and parents find loans, grants, scholarships, and work-study programs.

The Job

A college administrator's work is demanding and diverse. An administrator is responsible for a wide range of tasks in areas such as counseling services, admissions, alumni affairs, financial aid, academics, and business. The following are some of the different types of college administrators; but keep in mind that this is only a partial list. It takes many administrators in many different departments to run a college.

Many college and university administrators are known as *deans*. Deans are the administrative heads of specific divisions or groups within the university and are in charge of overseeing the activities and policies of that division. One type of dean is an *academic dean*. Academic deans are concerned with such issues as the requirements for a major, the courses offered, and the faculty hired within a specific academic department or division. The field of academic dean includes such titles as dean of the college of humanities, dean of social and behavioral sciences, and dean of the graduate school, just to name a few. The *dean of students* is responsible for the student-affairs program, often including such areas as student housing, organizations, clubs, and activities.

Registrars prepare class schedules and final exam schedules. They maintain computer records of student data, such as grades and degree requirements. They prepare school catalogs and student handbooks. Associate registrars assist in the running of the school registrar's office.

Recruiters visit high school campuses and college fairs to provide information about their school and to interest students in applying for admission. They develop relationships with high school administrators, and arrange to meet with counselors, students, and parents.

College financial aid administrators direct the scholarship, grant-in-aid, and loan programs that provide financial assistance to students and help them meet the costs of tuition, fees, books, and other living expenses. The administrator keeps students informed of the financial assistance available to them and helps answer student and parent questions and concerns. At smaller colleges, this work might be done by a single person, the *financial aid officer.* At larger colleges and universities, the staff might be bigger, and the financial aid officer will head a department and direct the activities of *financial aid counselors,* who handle most of the personal contact with students.

Other college administrators include *college admissions counselors* who review records, interview prospective students, and process applications for admission. *Alumni directors* oversee the alumni associations of colleges and universities. An alumni director maintains relationships with the graduates of the college primarily for fund-raising purposes. Such jobs as *university president, vice president,* and *provost* are among the most high-ranking college and university administrative positions.

Requirements

High School

A good, well-rounded education is important for anyone pursuing some of the top administrative positions. To prepare for a job in college administration, take accounting and math courses, as you may be dealing with financial records and student statistics. To be a dean of a college, you must have good communication skills; take courses in English literature and composition. Also, speech courses are important, as you'll be required to give presentations and to represent your department at meetings and conferences. Follow your guidance counselor's college preparatory plan, which will likely include courses in science, foreign languages, history, and sociology.

Postsecondary Training

Education requirements for jobs in college administration will depend on the size of the school and the job position. Some assistant positions may not require anything more than a few years experience in an office. For most jobs in college administration, however, you'll need at least a bachelor's degree; for the top administrative positions, you'll need a master's or a doctorate. A bachelor's degree in any field is usually acceptable for pursuing this career. After you've received your bachelor's, you may choose to pursue a master's in student personnel, administration, or subjects such as economics, psychology, and sociology. Other important studies include education, counseling, information processing, business, and finance. In order to become a college dean, you'll need a doctoral degree and many years of experience with a college or university. Your degree may be in your area of study or in college administration.

Other Requirements

You should be very organized and able to manage a busy office of assistants. Some offices require more organization than others; for example, a financial aid office handles the records and aid disbursement for the entire student body, and requires a director with an eye for efficiency and the ability to keep track of all the various sources of student funding. As a dean, however, you'll work in a smaller office, concentrating more on issues concerning faculty and committees, and you'll rely on your diplomatic skills for maintaining an efficient and successful department. People skills are valuable for college deans, as you'll be representing your department both within the university and at national conferences.

Whatever the administrative position, it is important to have patience and tact to handle a wide range of personalities as well as an emotional steadiness when confronted with unusual and unexpected situations.

Exploring

To learn something about what the job of administrator entails, you should talk to your principal and superintendent. Also, interview administrators at colleges and universities. Many of their office phone numbers are listed in college directories. The email addresses of the administrators of many different departments, from deans to registrars, are often published on college

Web sites. You could also discuss the career with the college recruiters who visit your high school. Also, familiarize yourself with all the various aspects of running a college and university by looking at college student handbooks and course catalogs. Most handbooks list all the offices and administrators and how they assist students and faculty.

Employers

Administrators are needed all across the country to run colleges and universities. Job opportunities exist at public and private institutions, community colleges, and universities both large and small. In a smaller college, an administrator may run more than one department. There are more job openings for administrators in universities serving large student bodies.

Starting Out

There are several different types of entry-level positions available in the typical college administrative office. If you can gain part-time work or an internship in admissions or another office while you are still in school, you will have a great advantage when seeking work in this field after graduation. Any other experience in an administrative or managerial position, which involves working with people or with computerized data, is also helpful. Entry-level positions often involve filing, data processing, and updating records or charts. You might also move into a position as an administrator after working as a college professor. Deans in colleges and universities have usually worked many years as tenured professors.

The department of human resources in most colleges and universities maintains a listing of job openings at the institution, and will often advertise the positions nationally. *The Chronicle of Higher Education* is a newspaper with national job listings. The College and University Professional Association for Human Resources also maintains a job list.

Advancement

Entry-level positions, which usually require only a bachelor's degree, include *admissions counselors,* who advise students regarding admissions requirements and decisions, and *evaluators,* who check high school transcripts and college transfer records to determine whether applying students may be admitted. *Administrative assistants* are hired for the offices of registrars, financial aid departments, and deans.

Advancement from any of these positions will depend on the manner in which an office is organized as well as how large it is. One may move up to assistant director or associate director, or, in a larger office, into any specialized divisions such as minority admissions, financial aid counseling, or disabled student services. Advancement also may come through transferring to other departments, schools, or systems.

Workshops and seminars are available through professional associations for those interested in staying informed and becoming more knowledgeable in the field, but it is highly unlikely that an office employee will gain the top administrative level without a graduate degree.

Earnings

Salaries for college administrators vary widely among two-year and four-year colleges and among public and private institutions, but are generally comparable to those of college faculty. Those in entry-level positions often earn less than $20,000 a year, but admissions and financial aid directors, and registrars, have average salaries of over $45,000. The salaries of deans also vary greatly between departments. According to the 1997-98 Administrative Compensation Survey conducted by the College and University Professional Association for Human Resources, the median salary for deans of medicine is $235,000 a year, while the median annual salary for deans of nursing is $76,380.

Most colleges and universities provide excellent benefits packages including health insurance, paid vacation, sick leave, and tuition remission. Higher level administrators such as presidents, deans, and provosts often receive such bonuses as access to special university clubs, tickets to sporting events, expense accounts for entertaining university guests, and other privileges.

Work Environment

The college or university environment is usually a pleasant place in which to be employed. Offices are often spacious and comfortable and the campus may be a scenic, relaxing work setting.

Employment in most administrative positions is usually on a 12-month basis. Many of the positions, such as admissions director, financial aid counselor, and dean of students, require a great deal of direct contact with students, and so working hours may vary according to student needs. It is not unusual to work long hours during peak enrollment periods, such as the beginning of each quarter or semester. During these periods, the office can be fast paced and stressful as administrators work to assist as many students as possible. Directors are sometimes required to work evenings and weekends to provide wider student access to administrative services. In addition, administrators are sometimes required to travel to other colleges, career fairs, high schools, and professional conferences to interview and provide information about the school for which they work.

Outlook

Although the U.S. Department of Labor predicts job openings, the department also predicts strong competition for the prestigious position of college administrator. Many faculty at institutions of higher learning have the educational and experience requirements for the job. In addition, budget cuts or budgets without growth have forced some institutions to reduce or consolidate administrative jobs. The employment outlook is expected to show little change through 2008. Applicants with the best chances of getting administrative positions will be those who are either willing to relocate or those who are already working within a department seeking an administrator.

For More Information

For information about publications, current legislation, and membership, contact the following organizations:

American Association of University Administrators
2602 Rutford Avenue
Richardson, TX 75080-1470
Tel: 972-248-3957
Web: http://www.aaua.org

College and University Professional Association for Human Resources
1233 20th Street, NW, Suite 301
Washington, DC 20036-1250
Tel: 202-429-0311
Web: http://www.cupahr.org

College Professors

English **History**	School Subjects
Communication/ideas **Helping/teaching**	Personal Skills
Primarily indoors **Primarily one location**	Work Environment
Master's degree	Minimum Education Level
$39,000 to $47,000 to $85,000	Salary Range
None available	Certification or Licensing
Faster than the average	Outlook

Overview

College professors instruct undergraduate and graduate students in specific subjects at colleges and universities. They are responsible for lecturing classes, leading small seminar groups, and creating and grading examinations. They also may carry on research, write for publication, and aid in administration.

History

The concept of a college or university goes back many centuries. These institutions evolved slowly from monastery schools, which trained a select few for certain professions, notably theology. The terms college and university have become virtually interchangeable in America outside the walls of academia, although originally they designated two very different kinds of institutions.

Two of the most notable early European universities were the University of Bologna in Italy, thought to have been established in the 12th century, and the University of Paris, which was chartered in 1201. These universities were considered to be models after which other European universities were patterned. Oxford University in England was probably established during the 12th century. Oxford served as a model for early American colleges and universities, and today is still considered one of the world's leading institutions.

Harvard, the first U.S. college, was established in 1636. Its stated purpose was to train men for the ministry. The early colleges were all established for religious training. With the growth of state-supported institutions in the early 18th century, the process of freeing the curriculum from ties with the church began. The University of Virginia established the first liberal arts curriculum in 1825 and these innovations were later adopted by many other colleges and universities.

Although the original colleges in the United States were patterned after Oxford University, they later came under the influence of German universities. During the 19th century, more than nine thousand Americans went to Germany to study. The emphasis in German universities was on scientific method. Most of the people who had studied in Germany returned to the United States to teach in universities, bringing this objective, factual approach to education and to other fields of learning.

In 1833, Oberlin College in Oberlin, Ohio, became the first college founded as a coeducational institution. In 1836 the first women-only college, Wesleyan Female College, was founded in Macon, Georgia.

The junior college movement in the United States has been one of the most rapidly growing educational developments. Junior colleges first came into being just after the turn of the 20th century.

The Job

College and university faculty members teach at junior colleges or at four-year colleges and universities. At four-year institutions, most faculty members are *assistant professors, associate professors,* or *full professors.* These three types of professorships differ in regards to status, job responsibilities, and salary. Assistant professors are new faculty members who are working to get tenure (status as a permanent professor); they seek to advance to associate and then to full professorships.

College professors perform three main functions: teaching, advising, and research. Their most important responsibility is to teach students. Their role within a college department will determine the level of courses they teach and the number of courses per semester. Most professors work with students at all levels, from college freshmen to graduate students. They may head several classes a semester, or only a few a year. Some of their classes will have large enrollment, while graduate seminars may only consist of 12 or fewer students. Though college professors may spend fewer than 10 hours a week in the actual classroom, they spend many hours preparing lectures and lesson plans, grading papers and exams, and preparing grade reports. They also schedule office hours during the week to be available to students outside of the lecture hall, and they meet with students individually throughout the semester. In the classroom, professors lecture, lead discussions, administer exams, and assign textbook reading and other research. In some courses, they rely heavily on laboratories to transmit course material.

Another important responsibility is advising students. Not all faculty members serve as advisers, but those who do must set aside large blocks of time to guide students through the program. College professors who serve as advisers may have any number of students assigned to them, from fewer than 10 to more than 100, depending on the administrative policies of the college. Their responsibility may involve looking over a planned program of studies to make sure the students meet requirements for graduation, or it may involve working intensively with each student on many aspects of college life.

The third responsibility of college and university faculty members is research and publication. Faculty members who are heavily involved in research programs sometimes are assigned a smaller teaching load. College professors publish their research findings in various scholarly journals. They also write books based on their research or on their own knowledge and experience in the field. Most textbooks are written by college and university teachers. In arts-based programs, such as master's of fine arts programs in painting, writing, and theater, professors practice their craft and exhibit their art work in various ways. For example, a painter or photographer will have gallery showings, while a poet will publish in literary journals.

Publishing a significant amount of work has been the traditional standard by which assistant professors prove themselves worthy of becoming permanent, tenured faculty. Typically, pressure to publish is greatest for assistant professors. Pressure to publish increases again if an associate professor wishes to be considered for a promotion to full professorship.

In recent years, some liberal arts colleges have recognized that the pressure to publish is taking faculty away from their primary duties to the students, and these institutions have begun to place a decreasing emphasis on publishing and more on performance in the classroom. Professors in junior colleges face less pressure to publish than those in four-year institutions.

Some faculty members eventually rise to the position of *department chair,* where they govern the affairs of an entire department, such as English, mathematics, or biological sciences. Department chairs, faculty, and other professional staff members are aided in their myriad duties by *graduate assistants,* who may help develop teaching materials, conduct research, give examinations, teach lower-level courses, and carry out other activities.

Some college professors may also conduct classes in an extension program. In such a program, they teach evening and weekend courses for the benefit of people who otherwise would not be able to take advantage of the institution's resources. They may travel away from the campus and meet with a group of students at another location. They may work full time for the extension division, or may divide the time between on-campus and off-campus teaching.

An *extension work instructor* teaches through correspondence courses usually available only to undergraduate students. In a standard course of study for the subject, a college professor's responsibility would be to grade the papers that the student sends in at periodic intervals and to advise the student of progress. Extension work instructors may perform this service in addition to other duties or may be assigned to correspondence work as a major teaching responsibility.

The *junior college instructor* has many of the same kinds of responsibilities as does the teacher in a four-year college or university. Because junior colleges offer only a two-year program, they only teach undergraduates.

Requirements

High School

Your high school's college-preparatory program likely includes courses in English, science, foreign language, math, and government. In addition, you should take courses in speech to get a sense of what it will be like to lecture to a group of students. Your school's debate team can also help you develop public speaking skills, along with research skills.

Postsecondary Training

At least one advanced degree in your field of study is required to be a professor in a college or university. The master's degree is considered the minimum standard, and graduate work beyond the master's is usually desirable. A doctorate is required to advance in academic rank above instructor in most institutions.

In the last year of your undergraduate program, you'll apply to graduate programs in your area of study. Standards for admission to a graduate program can be high, and the competition heavy, depending on the school. Once accepted into a program, your responsibilities will be similar to those of your professors—in addition to attending seminars, you'll research, prepare articles for publication, and teach some undergraduate courses.

The faculty member in a junior college may be employed with only a master's degree. Advancement in responsibility and in salary, however, is more likely to come to those who have earned a doctorate.

Other Requirements

You should enjoy reading, writing, and researching. Not only will you spend many years studying in school, but your whole career will be based on communicating your thoughts and ideas. People skills are important because you'll be dealing directly with students, administrators, and other faculty members on a daily basis. You should feel comfortable in a role of authority, and possess self-confidence.

Exploring

Your high school teachers use many of the same skills as college professors, so talk to your teachers about their careers and their college experiences. You can develop your own teaching experience by volunteering with a community center, working at a daycare center, or working at a summer camp. Also, spend some time on a college campus to get a sense of the environment. Write to colleges for their admissions brochures and course catalogs; read about the faculty members and the courses they teach. Before visiting college campuses, make arrangements to speak to professors who teach courses that interest you. These professors may allow you to sit in on their classes and observe. Also, make appointments with college advisers, and with people in the admissions and recruitment offices.

Employers

Employment opportunities vary based on area of study and education. Most universities have many different departments that hire faculty. With a doctorate, a number of publications, and a record of good teaching, professors should find opportunities in universities all across the country: there are more than 3,800 colleges and universities in the United States. Professors teach in undergraduate and graduate programs. The teaching jobs at doctoral institutions are usually better paying and more prestigious. The most sought-after positions are those that offer tenure. Teachers that only have a master's degree will be limited to opportunities with junior colleges, community colleges, and some small private institutions.

Starting Out

While in graduate school, you'll be working toward developing your curriculum vitae (a detailed, academic resume). You'll write for publication, assist with research, attend conferences, and gain teaching experience and recommendations. While finishing your graduate program, you'll apply for teaching positions. For most positions at four-year institutions, you'll have to travel to large conferences where you'll be interviewed by several professors from the universities to which you have applied.

Because of the competition for tenure-track positions, you may have to work for a few years in temporary positions, visiting various schools as an *adjunct professor*. Some professional associations maintain lists of teaching opportunities in their areas. They may also make lists of applicants available to college administrators looking to fill an available position.

Advancement

The normal pattern of advancement is from instructor to assistant professor, to associate professor, to full professor. All four academic ranks are concerned primarily with teaching and research. College faculty members who have an interest in and a talent for administration may be advanced to chair of a department, or to dean of their college. A few become college or university presidents or other types of administrators.

The instructor is usually an inexperienced college teacher. He or she may hold a doctorate or may have completed all the Ph.D. requirements except for the dissertation. Most colleges look upon the rank of instructor as the period during which the college is trying the teacher out. Instructors usually are advanced to the position of assistant professors within three to four years. Assistant professors are given up to about six years to prove themselves worthy of tenure, and if they do so, they become associate professors. Some professors choose to remain at the associate level. Others strive to become full professors and receive greater status, salary, and responsibilities.

Most colleges have clearly defined promotion policies from rank to rank for faculty members and many have written statements about the number of years in which instructors and assistant professors may remain in grade. Administrators in many colleges hope to encourage younger faculty members to increase their skills and competencies and thus to qualify for the more responsible positions of associate professor and full professor.

Earnings

Both the *Chronicle of Higher Education* and the American Association of University Professors (AAUP) conduct annual surveys of the salaries of college professors. With the 1998 survey, the *Chronicle* found that full professors at public universities received an average of $69,924 a year, while professors at private universities received $84,970 a year. Associate professors received an average of $50,186 annually at public universities, and $56,517 at private universities. For assistant professors, the average salaries were $42,335 public, $47,387 private.

The AAUP's 1999 survey found that salary levels had increased from the previous year, but remain 4.4 percent lower than 25 years ago, when figures are adjusted for inflation. Professors earn 42 percent less than those in comparable professions. The AAUP survey found that professors in doctoral institutions made an average of $66,991 a year, compared to $53,454 for those in master's institutions, and $48,257 for those in undergraduate institutions. Professors working in the West Coast states, such as California and Oregon, earned the most, followed by those working in New England. The survey found the average pay to be the lowest in such southern states as Alabama, Kentucky, and Mississippi.

Work Environment

A college or university is usually a pleasant place in which to work. Campuses bustle with all types of activities and events, stimulating ideas, and a young, energetic population. Much prestige comes with success as a professor and scholar; professors have the respect of students, colleagues, and others in their community.

Depending on the size of the department, college professors may have their own office, or they may have to share an office with one or more colleagues. Their department may provide them with a computer, Internet access, and research assistants. College professors are also able to do much of their office work at home. They can arrange their schedule around class hours, academic meetings, and the established office hours when they meet with students. Most college teachers work more than 40 hours each week. Although college professors may only teach two or three classes a semester, they spend many hours preparing for lectures, examining student work, and conducting research.

Outlook

The U.S. Department of Labor predicts faster than average growth for college and university professors through 2008. College enrollment is projected to rise from 14.6 million in 1998 to 16.1 million in 2008, an increase of about 10 percent. Competition for jobs, especially full-time, tenure-track positions at 4-year universities, will be very strong. Additionally, opportunities for college teachers will be good in areas that offer strong career prospects in the world of work, such as engineering, business, computer science, and health science.

A number of factors threaten to change the way colleges and universities hire faculty. Some university leaders are developing more business-based methods of running their schools, focusing on profits and budgets. This can affect college professors in a number of ways. One of the biggest effects is in the replacement of tenure-track faculty positions with part-time instructors. These part-time instructors include adjunct faculty, visiting professors, and graduate students. Organizations such as the American Association of University Professors and the American Federation of Teachers are working to prevent the loss of these full-time jobs, as well as to help part-time instructors receive better pay and benefits. Other issues involve the development of long-distance education departments in many schools. Though these correspondence courses have become very popular in recent years, many professionals believe that students in long-distance education programs receive only a second-rate education. A related concern is about the proliferation of computers in the classroom. Some courses consist only of instruction by computer software and the Internet. The effects of these alternative methods on the teaching profession will be offset somewhat by the expected increases in college enrollment in coming years.

For More Information

To read about the issues affecting college professors, contact the following organizations:

American Association of University Professors
1012 14th Street, NW, Suite 500
Washington, DC 20005-3465
Tel: 202-737-5900
Email: aaup@aaup.org
Web: http://www.aaup.org

American Federation of Teachers
555 New Jersey Avenue, NW
Washington, DC 20001
Tel: 202-879-4400
Web: http://www.aft.org

Computer Trainers

Computer science Speech	School Subjects
Helping/teaching Technical/scientific	Personal Skills
Primarily indoors Primarily multiple locations	Work Environment
Bachelor's degree	Minimum Education Level
$36,500 to $47,400 to $57,800	Salary Range
Recommended	Certification or Licensing
Much faster than the average	Outlook

Overview

Computer trainers teach topics related to all aspects of using computers in the workplace, including personal computer (PC) software; operating systems for both stand-alone and networked systems; management tools for networks; enterprise software that enables efficient management of large corporations' production, sales, and information systems; software applications and operating systems for mainframe computers and customized software for specific industry management. Some trainers work for training companies, and others for software developers. They also work for companies that produce training materials, including disk-based multimedia technology-delivered learning, instructor-led courseware, skills assessment, videos, and classroom teaching manuals.

History

The worldwide market for information technology (IT) education and training was estimated at $18.8 billion in 1998, up from $14.7 billion in 1996, according to International Data Corporation. Computer skills training was ranked the leading training category in 1997 by a national executive survey and was forecasted to continue to place in the top three for years to come, according to the American Society for Training and Development (ASTD).

The field of computer training has been around since about 1983, when the computer industry exploded with the introduction of the first PCs. With all of the new software packages being released, individual IT and information services (IS) departments could not possibly keep up with the amount of training their employees needed. Software vendor companies started sending their employees out to teach new purchasers how to use their products, and a new section of the computer industry was born.

In the beginning, computer training was conducted like any other training, in a classroom setting with an instructor. Although that type of training is still prevalent today, "Now, that landscape is awash with a torrent of new technologies, creating almost limitless possibilities for heightened learning," according to "Training Industry Trends 1997," by Laurie J. Bassi, Scott Cheney, and Mark Van Buren of the ASTD. "These days, a variety of electronic media can facilitate the transfer of knowledge and skills. That represents both a challenge and an opportunity for professionals who specialize in workplace learning and performance. Technological innovation is constantly and pervasively altering the way in which work is done. That, in turn, has immediate consequences for the demands on specialists in workplace learning and performance improvement. The rapid pace of change requires that workplace learning occur on a just-in-time, just-what's-needed, and just-where-it's-needed basis."

Computer trainers are turning to that technology to deliver their instructions. Developments in hardware, computer networking, multimedia software, and video conferencing have tremendous potential for multiple-site instruction and training closer to people's work sites, according to the ASTD. The organization also notes that training departments are finding new ways to deliver services, by using support networks of internal and external training providers, including consultants, community colleges, and universities.

The Job

The field of computer training encompasses several different areas. *Software vendor trainers* work for developer companies. *Consultants* work for themselves as independent contractors, often specializing in certain computer languages, skills, or platforms. Some trainers work in the corporate training departments of companies that develop products other than computers and software. Others are teachers and professors.

"As a software trainer, my duties are to be prepared to teach various topics related to our software to a variety of clients on any given day," says Marcy Anderson, a software trainer for Cyborg Systems, a human-resource software developer. "I teach from a training manual and demonstrate the procedures on my computer that displays the information on a large screen for the entire class. The class is given assignments throughout the day that they complete on their PCs. I assist them one on one with their questions as the class continues. Cyborg has a training center with four classrooms. I conduct classes in the training center, or I travel to the client and hold classes on-site."

Consultant trainers are certified to teach several different products, applications, environments, and databases, usually with companies such as Microsoft, IBM, or Apple. Most have been in the computer industry for many years, previously working as software programmers, architects, project managers, or developers.

Whatever their affiliation, most computer trainers use several ways to disseminate learning technologies, including CD-ROM, CBT-Text, electronic performance support systems, the Internet, Intranets, multimedia presentations, and video conferencing.

One of the most important things for trainers to have is certification for the courses they intend to instruct. The International Board of Standards for Training, Performance, and Instruction has an outline of ground-level skills that are mandatory for technical trainers, according to the ASTD. The following 14 competencies are the basis for the certified trainer examination. For trainers to receive certification, they must show proof that they can execute the following:

1. Analyze course materials and learning information.
2. Ensure preparation of the instructional site.
3. Establish and maintain instructor credibility.
4. Manage the learning environment.
5. Demonstrate effective communication skills.
6. Demonstrate effective presentation skills.
7. Demonstrate effective questioning skills and techniques.
8. Respond appropriately to learners' needs for clarification or feedback.
9. Provide positive reinforcement and motivational incentives.

10. Use instructional methods appropriately.
11. Use media effectively.
12. Evaluate learner performance.
13. Evaluate instruction delivery.
14. Report evaluation information.

Trainers are beginning to explore the field of online learning. In the article, "Our Turn-of-the-Century Trend Watch," Paul Clothier, senior instructor, Softwire Corporation, says that "improved online learning (OL) design and technologies will significantly impact the technical training profession over the next few years. At present, much of the technical training taking place is in the form of instructor-led training (ILT) in a classroom. There are many advantages to ILT, but there are also considerable disadvantages, such as time investment, travel, and expense. To get a group of your most valuable technical people off to a week of training is often a major expense and inconvenience. Organizations are crying out for a better alternative, and OL increasingly is seen as an option."

Requirements

High School

If you are interested in a career in computer training, take as many computer and mathematics classes as possible in high school. These will provide the foundation for the rest of your computer education. Start learning about computer programs, such as Visual Basic, on your own. Speech, drama, or other performance courses will also help get you used to speaking in front of a crowd. "A little showmanship doesn't hurt in keeping the class interested," notes Marcy Anderson.

Postsecondary Training

While there is no universally accepted way to prepare for a job in computer training, a bachelor's degree is generally required from most employers, but it is not set in stone which major is the best one for this field. Some majors that share skills with training include computer science, business, and education. To teach some of the more complex systems, a graduate degree might be necessary.

"In my personal experience, I did not pursue an education degree to become a trainer," says Anderson. "I have a business degree and years of experience in the human resources field. For software training, though, knowledge of software and computers is essential. A degree in education would provide excellent skills for this type of position. Additionally, a business or liberal arts major might provide the presentation skills that are valuable. Certainly any presentation or public speaking certifications would be desirable."

Obtaining graduate and postgraduate degrees enhances potential marketability, as well as future salaries.

Certification or Licensing

Trainers should be certified in the products (such as Microsoft C++, MFC, Visual Basic, and Access), developments (including Internet, HTML, Java Script), applications (MS Office, for example), environments (such as OS/2, Windows, client/server), and databases (including ADO, Access, ODBC, BD/2, and SQL) they want to instruct. Classes in each of the disciplines are available from the manufacturers, and students must pass an examination before receiving certification. Trainers who are employed by hardware and software developers might receive on-the-job instruction on the most current product releases. Certification is not mandatory (except for consultants), but it will provide job seekers with competitive advantages. The International Association of Information Technology Trainers awards the Professional Technical Trainer designation to association members who complete a seminar, submit a 30-minute video of one of their training presentations, and pay an application fee. Additionally, applicants must provide 10 student references and post-class evaluations.

Technological advances come so rapidly in the computer field that continuous study even for trainers is necessary to keep skills up to date. Continuing education is usually offered by employers, hardware and software vendors, colleges and universities, or private training institutions. Additional training can also come from professional associations, such as the American Society for Training and Development.

Other Requirements

"Trainers need to be patient and extroverted," says Marcy Anderson. "A sense of humor is essential, along with a high level of energy. People who are very introverted, even though they might be good with computers, should not do software training." Trainers also have to be ready to teach any class in their repertoire at any time, so they have to be adaptable and flexible to handle that uncertainty.

Exploring

One way to begin exploring this field now is to talk to someone who is a computer trainer. Anderson also suggests getting involved in speech or drama clubs. "Any experiences a high schooler can get in making presentations or performing in front of a group help to build the skills necessary to be successful in this career," she says.

Internships are always helpful ways of obtaining some experience in the field before graduation. Having a job in the training department of a large corporation or software vendor would provide invaluable experience and contacts.

Teach yourself the various software packages, and read as much as you can about the industry. Although jobs in the computer industry are abundant, there is always competition for desirable positions.

Employers

Computer trainers are employed by various sources, from large, international companies to community colleges. Many work for hardware and software manufacturers or training departments in the bigger companies. Others are employed by training companies that disseminate training information and tools. Still other computer trainers work independently as consultants. The rest are employed by schools, adult continuing education programs, and government institutions. Some software companies and consultants operate training sites on the Internet. Since almost every type of company will need computer training at one point or another, these companies are located throughout the country, and, indeed, throughout the world.

Starting Out

There are several ways to obtain a position as a computer trainer. Some people are hired right out of college by software companies. "There are many software companies that hire smart college grads to work with clients and implement their software," notes Anderson. Others start out in technical positions with software companies and then move into training as their expertise in the product increases.

Job candidates for computer trainer positions might obtain their jobs from on-campus recruitment, classified want ads, posting their resume on the Internet, or word of mouth. Many large cities hold technology job fairs that host hundreds of companies, all of which are interested in hiring.

Advancement

Depending on the size of the company, trainers can advance into positions such as training specialists, senior training specialists, and training managers.

Earnings

The average training specialist earned $40,300 in 1996, according to the Information Systems Compensation Survey, compiled by William M. Mercer Inc. Senior training specialists averaged $47,400 per year, and training managers earned $57,000. In general, salaries in the area of computer trainers increased with the level of education. The average salary for managers with postgraduate degrees was significantly higher than average, totaling $47,863, according to the 1999 *Service News* Salary Survey.

Most computer trainers who are employed by corporations receive medical and dental insurance, paid vacations, sick days, and yearly bonuses. In 1996, bonuses for training specialists averaged $1,600, senior training specialists received $2,500, and training managers were awarded $5,200 on average.

Work Environment

Computer trainers normally work in offices in comfortable surroundings. They usually work 40 hours a week, which is the same as many other professional or office workers. However, travel to clients' sites can be required and might increase the number of hours worked per week. They spend most of their time in classrooms or training facilities. "The best part of the job is that it is interesting and fun," says Marcy Anderson. "It is nice to be an 'expert' and impart knowledge to others, even though it can be hard sometimes to feel up and energized to teach every day."

Outlook

The field of computers is expected to grow much faster than average through 2008. Consequently, there will be a great need for computer trainers as the technology continues to develop. Information from the National Center on the Educational Quality of the Workforce indicates that employers are using a variety of external training providers. As this outsourcing grows, an increase in the number of training providers is likely. Such independent providers as community and technical colleges, universities, profit-oriented learning and development centers, and private industry associations will all be discovering new business opportunities in outsourcing, according to the American Society for Training and Development (ASTD). "The short life cycles of technology products, compounded by the greater complexity of many job roles, are expected to heighten the demand for external information-technology education providers and other training providers," the ASTD notes.

For More Information

For a list of academic programs and resources in the computer training field, contact the following organizations:

American Society for Training and Development
1640 King Street, Box 1443
Alexandria, VA 22313-2043
Tel: 800-628-2783
Email: customercare@astd.org
Web: http://www.astd.org

International Association of Information Technology Trainers
PMB 451
6030-M Marshalee Drive
Elkridge, MD 21075-5935
Tel: 888-290-6200
Web: http://itrain.org

Education Directors

School Subjects

English
Speech

Personal Skills

Communication/ideas
Helping/teaching

Work Environment

Primarily indoors
One location with some travel

Minimum Education Level

Bachelor's degree

Salary Range

$23,000 to $35,000 to $56,000+

Certification or Licensing

None available

Outlook

Little change or more slowly
than the average

Overview

Museums, zoos, and botanical gardens are visited by people who come to learn and observe. *Education directors* are responsible for helping these people enrich their visits. Education directors plan, develop, and administer educational programs at museums and other similar institutions. They plan tours, lectures, and classes for individuals, school groups, and special interest groups.

History

In early times, churches displayed art and furnishings for worshipers to view. The early equivalents of education directors were the priests or laypeople who developed expertise in the collections. As public museums grew, so did their need for education directors. When Europeans began to encourage the idea of universal education, museums began to draw in uneducated visitors who needed to be taught about their collections.

Similarly, zoos and arboretums, which were originally organized to exhibit their animals and plants to experts, began to teach others about their collections. Education directors were hired to plan programs and tours for visitors.

In the United States, early museums displayed objects relating to colonial history. Some were in former homes of wealthy colonists and others were established at the first U.S. universities and colleges. In these early museums curators or archivists maintained the collections and also explained the collections to visitors. As the collections grew and more visitors and groups of visitors came, education directors were hired by the curators to coordinate educational programs.

The Job

Education directors carry out the educational goals of a museum, zoo, botanical garden, or other similar institution. The educational goals of most of these institutions include nurturing curiosity and answering questions of visitors, regardless of age or background. Education directors work with administrators and museum or zoo boards to determine the scope of their educational programs. Large museums may offer full schedules of classes and tours, while smaller ones may only provide tours or lectures at the request of a school or other group.

Education directors plan schedules of courses to be offered through the zoo or museum. They may hire lecturers from local colleges or universities as well as regular educational staff members to lead tours or discussion groups. Education directors are usually responsible for training the staff members and may also work with professionals or university faculty to determine the content of a particular lecture, class, or series of lectures. They prepare course outlines and establish the credentials necessary for those who will teach the courses.

In smaller institutions the education director may do much of the teaching, lecturing, or tour leading. In zoos, the education director can arrange for small children to watch cows being milked or for the children to pet or feed such smaller animals as goats. In museums, the education director's job often depends on the museum's collection. In art museums, visitors are often older than in natural history museums, and the education director may plan programs that allow older children to explore parts of the collection at their own pace.

Education directors often promote their programs on local radio or television or in newspapers. They may speak to community or school groups about the museum's education department and encourage the groups to attend. Sometimes, education directors deliver lectures or offer classes away from the museum or zoo.

The education director is responsible for the budget for all educational programs. Directors prepare budgets and supervise the records of income and spending. Often, schools or other groups are charged lower rates for tours or classes at museums or zoos. Education directors work with resource coordinators to establish budgets for resource materials. These need to be updated regularly in most institutions. Even in natural history museums, where the collections may change less than in other museums, slide collections may need to be updated or presentations altered if new research has led to different interpretations of the objects. The education director may also prepare grant proposals or help with fund-raising efforts for the museum's educational program. Once a grant has been received or a large gift has been offered to the education department, the education director plans for the best use of the funds within the department.

Education directors train their staff members as well as volunteers to work with individual visitors and groups. Some volunteers may be trained to assist in presentations or to help large groups on tours. It is the responsibility of the educational director to see that the educational program is helpful and interesting to all of the various people who visit the museum or zoo.

Special activities planned by educational directors vary widely depending on the institution. Film programs, filed trips, lectures, and full-day school programs may be offered weekly, monthly, or annually. Some zoos and arboretums have ongoing tours offered daily, while others may only give tours for prearranged groups.

Educational resource coordinators work with education directors. They are responsible for the collection of education materials used in the educational programs. These may include slides, posters, videotapes, books, or materials for special projects. Educational resource coordinators prepare, buy, catalog, and maintain all of the materials used by the education department. They sometimes have a lending library of films, videos, books, or slides that people may borrow. Resource coordinators keep track of the circulation of materials. They may also lead tours or workshops for educators or school personnel to teach them about the collection of the museum or zoo and to keep them apprised of new materials the educators may use in their tours or in their own classrooms. Resource coordinators and directors attend conventions and teachers' meetings to promote their institution's educational program and to encourage participation in their classes or tours.

Education directors often work with *exhibit designers* to help create displays that are most effective for visitors. They may also work with illustrators to produce illustrations or signs that enhance exhibits. Zoos, for example, often display maps near the animals to show their countries of origin.

Requirements

High School

Education directors, as well as the majority of museum professionals, need diverse educational backgrounds to perform well in their jobs. At the high school level, you should take courses in creative writing, literature, history of world civilizations, American history, the sciences, foreign languages, art, and speech. These courses will give you general background knowledge you can use to interpret collections, write letters to school principals, design curriculum materials, develop multicultural education, and lecture to public audiences. Math and computer skills are also strongly recommended. Education directors use these skills when preparing budgets, calculating the number of visitors that can fit in an exhibit space, and when writing grants or asking corporations and federal agencies for program funding.

Postsecondary Training

Education directors must have a bachelor's degree. Many museums, zoos, and botanical gardens also require a master's degree. The largest zoos and museums prefer to hire education directors who have doctoral degrees. Most education directors work in museums that specialize in art, history, or science. These directors often have degrees in fields related to the museum's specialty. Those who work in zoos usually have studied biology or zoology or have worked closely with animals. Education directors who work in more specialized museums often have studied such specialized fields as early American art, woodcarvings, or the history of circuses. All education directors must have a good working knowledge of the animals, plants, or artifacts in their collection.

Other Requirements

Excellent communication skills are essential. Education directors have a primary responsibility to interpret and present their collections to a broad public audience. The ability to motivate and teach many individuals from a wide range of cultural backgrounds, age groups, and educational levels is necessary. Education directors should be organized and flexible.

Exploring

Volunteer experience for students interested in becoming education directors is easy to obtain. Most zoos and museums have student volunteers. High school students can request a position in the education department. They may help with elementary school tours, organize files or audiovisual materials, or assist a lecturer in a class.

College-preparatory courses are important for students interested in the field. They should apply to colleges or universities with strong liberal arts programs. Courses in art, history, science, and education are recommended for those who want to work at museums. Courses in biology, zoology, botany, and education are beneficial for those who wish to work at zoos or botanical gardens. Some larger zoos and museums offer internships to college students who are interested in the field.

The American Association of Museums publishes an annual museum directory, a monthly newsletter, and a bimonthly magazine. It also published *Museum Careers: A Variety of Vocations.* This report is helpful for anyone considering a career in the museum field. *Introduction to Museum Work,* published by the American Association for State and Local History, discusses the educational programs at various museums. Also, the American Association of Botanical Gardens and Arboreta publishes a directory of over 500 internships offered through public gardens each year.

Employers

Institutions with a primary goal to educate the public about their collections hire education directors. Depending on each institution's monetary resources, most museums, large and small, zoos, botanical gardens, and occasionally, historical societies employ education directors to ensure public access to their collections. Institutions with small operating budgets or limited visitor access sometimes hire part-time educators or rely on volunteer support.

Starting Out

Students who wish to become education directors must get a bachelor's degree. Their first job in a museum or zoo is usually as a teacher or resource coordinator working in the education department. With a few years of experience and improved understanding of the institution's collection, they may choose to enter competition for promotion to education director. Many people in the field transfer from one museum to another or from one zoo to another, in order to be promoted to the position of education director.

Advancement

Once in the education department, most people learn much of their work on the job. Experience in working with different people and groups becomes very important. Education directors must continually improve their understanding of their own institution's collection so that they can present it to school and other groups in the best way possible. Some education directors work for the federal government in specific subject areas such as aeronautics, philately, or science and technology. They must be proficient in these fields as well as in education.

After two to four years in the education department, depending on the institution, most museums and zoos allow people to apply for education director positions. Some require advanced degrees first. Others only require proficiency in the collection and proven ability to coordinate educational programs.

Earnings

Salaries for education directors vary widely depending on the size, type, and location of the institution, as well as the education and experience of the director. The average beginning salary for education directors with bachelor's degrees and one year of experience is $23,000. Those with master's degrees may earn starting salaries of $33,000. The Association of Art Museum Directors reports that the average salaries for education directors are from $35,000 to $56,000 annually. Some larger or better-funded zoos and museums pay significantly more, while others hire part-time education directors who may earn as little as $6,000 annually. Fringe benefits, including medical and dental insurance, paid vacations and sick leave, and retirement plans, vary according to each employer's policies.

Work Environment

Most people who choose to be education directors like to be in museums, botanical gardens, or zoos. They also enjoy teaching, planning activities, organizing projects, and carrying a great deal of responsibility. Those in zoos usually enjoy animals and like being outdoors. Those in museums like the quiet of a natural history museum or the energy and life of a science museum aimed at children. Educational directors should enjoy being in an academic environment where they work closely with scholars, researchers, and scientists.

Outlook

The employment outlook for education directors is expected to increase more slowly than average through 2008. Budget cutbacks have affected many museums and other cultural institutions, which have in turn reduced the size of their education departments. Many educators with specialties in sciences, the arts, or zoology are interested in becoming education directors at museums and zoos. Competition is especially intense for positions in large cities and those with more prestigious reputations. Some smaller museums and botanical gardens may cut out their education director position altogether until the economic climate improves, or they may get by with part-time education directors.

For More Information

For information about publications, meetings, seminars, and workshops, contact:

American Association for State and Local History
1717 Church Street
Nashville, TN 37203-2991
Tel: 615-320-3203
Email: history@aaslh.org
Web: http://www.aaslh.org

For a directory of internships offered through public gardens, contact:

American Association of Botanical Gardens and Arboreta
351 Longwood Road
Kenneth Square, PA 19348
Tel: 610-925-2500
Web: http://www.aabga.org

For a directory of museums and other information, contact:

American Association of Museums
1575 Eye Street, NW, Suite 400
Washington, DC 20005
Tel: 202-289-1818
Web: http://www.aam-us.org

Elementary School Teachers

English Speech	School Subjects
Communication/ideas Helping/teaching	Personal Skills
Primarily indoors Primarily one location	Work Environment
Bachelor's degree	Minimum Education Level
$19,710 to $35,740 to $70,030	Salary Range
Required by all states	Certification or Licensing
About as fast as the average	Outlook

Overview

Elementary school teachers instruct students from the first through sixth or eighth grades. They develop teaching outlines and lesson plans, give lectures, facilitate discussions and activities, keep class attendance records, assign homework, and evaluate student progress. Most teachers work with one group of children throughout the day, teaching several subjects and supervising such activities as lunch and recess. Over 1 million kindergarten and elementary school teachers are employed in the United States.

History

The history of elementary education can be traced back to about 100 BC, when the people of Judah established schools for young children as part of their religious training.

In the early days of Western elementary education, the teacher only had to have completed elementary school to be considered qualified to teach. There was little incentive for an elementary school teacher to seek further education. School terms were generally short (about six months) and buildings were often cramped and poorly heated. Many elementary schools combined the entire eight grades into one room, teaching the same course of study for all ages. In these earliest schools, teachers were not well paid and had little status or recognition in the community.

When people began to realize that teachers should be better educated, schools designed to train teachers, called normal schools, were established. The first normal school was private and opened in Concord, Vermont, in 1823. The first state-supported normal school was established in Lexington, Massachusetts, in 1839. By 1900, nearly every state had at least one state-supported normal school.

The forerunner of the present-day college or school of education in large universities was the normal department established at Indiana University in 1852. Normal schools have since then given way to teachers' colleges and today almost every university in the country has a school or college of education.

The Job

Depending on the school, elementary school teachers teach grades one through six or eight. In smaller schools, grades may be combined. There are still a few one-room, one-teacher elementary schools in remote rural areas. However, in most cases, teachers instruct approximately 20 to 30 children of the same grade. They teach a variety of subjects in the prescribed course of study, including language, science, mathematics, and social studies. In the classroom, teachers use various methods to educate their students, ranging from reading to them, assigning group projects, and showing films for discussion. Teachers also use educational games to help their pupils come up with creative ways to remember lessons.

In the first and second grades, elementary school teachers cover the basic skills: reading, writing, counting, and telling time. With older students, teachers instruct history, geography, math, English, and handwriting. To capture attention and teach new concepts, they use arts and crafts projects, workbooks, music, and other interactive activities. In the upper grades, teachers assign written and oral reports and involve students in projects and competitions such as spelling bees, science fairs, and math contests. Although they are usually required to follow a curriculum designed by state or local administrators, teachers study new learning methods to incorporate into the classroom, such as using computers to surf the Internet.

"I utilize many different, some unorthodox, teaching tools," says Andrea LoCastro, a sixth-grade teacher in Clayton, New Jersey. "I have a lunchtime chess club. Students give up their recess to listen to classical music and play, or learn to play, chess." She has also found that role-playing activities keep her students interested in the various subjects. "We are studying ancient Greece," she says, "and I currently have my students writing persuasive essays as either part of Odysseus' legal team or the Cyclops' legal team. I intend to culminate the activity with a mock trial, Athenian style."

To create unique exercises and activities such as those LoCastro uses, teachers need to devote a fair amount of time to preparation outside of the classroom. They prepare daily lesson plans and assignments, grade papers and tests, and keep a record of each student's progress. Other responsibilities include communicating with parents through written reports and scheduled meetings, keeping their classroom orderly, and decorating desks and bulletin boards to keep the learning environment visually stimulating.

Elementary school teachers may also teach music, art, and physical education, but these areas are often covered by specialized teachers. *Art teachers* are responsible for developing art projects, procuring supplies, and helping students develop drawing, painting, sculpture, mural design, ceramics, and other artistic abilities. Some art teachers also teach students about the history of art and lead field trips to local museums. *Music teachers* teach music appreciation and history. They direct organized student groups such as choruses, bands, or orchestras, or guide music classes by accompanying them in singing songs or playing instruments. Often, music teachers are responsible for organizing school pageants, musicals, and plays. *Physical education teachers* help students develop physical skills such as coordination, strength, and stamina, and social skills such as self-confidence and good sportsmanship. Physical education teachers often serve as sports coaches and may be responsible for organizing field days and intramural activities.

When working with elementary-aged children, teachers need to instruct social skills along with general school subjects. They serve as disciplinarians, establishing and enforcing rules of conduct to help students learn right from wrong. To keep the classroom manageable, teachers maintain a system of rewards and punishments to encourage students to behave, stay interested, and participate. In cases of classroom disputes, teachers must also be mediators, teaching their pupils to peacefully work through arguments.

Recent developments in school curricula have led to new teaching arrangements and methods. In some schools, one or more teachers work with students within a small age range instead of with particular grades. Other schools are adopting bilingual education, where students are instructed throughout the day in two languages by either a *bilingual teacher* or two separate teachers.

Many teaching find it rewarding to witness students develop and hone new skills and adopt an appreciation for learning. In fact, many teachers inspire their own students to later join the teaching profession themselves. "Teaching is not just a career," says LoCastro, "it is a commitment: a commitment to the 20-plus children that walk into your classroom door each September eager for enlightenment and fun."

Requirements

High School

Follow your school's college preparatory program and take advanced courses in English, mathematics, science, history, and government to prepare for an education degree. Art, music, physical education, and extracurricular activities will contribute to a broad base of knowledge necessary to teach a variety of subjects. Composition, journalism, and communications classes are also important for developing your writing and speaking skills.

Postsecondary Training

All 50 states and the District of Columbia require public elementary education teachers to have a bachelor's degree in either education or in the subject they plan to teach, and to have completed an approved training program. In the United States, there are over 500 accredited teacher education programs, which combine subject and educational classes with work experience in the classroom.

Though programs vary by state, courses cover how to instruct language arts, mathematics, physical science, social science, art, and music. Additionally, prospective teachers must take educational training courses, such as philosophy of education, child psychology, and learning methods. To gain experience in the classroom, teachers-in-training are placed in a school to work with a full-time teacher. During their period of student teaching, they observe the ways in which lessons are presented and the classroom is managed, learn how to keep records of attendance and grades, and gain experience in handling the class, both under supervision and alone.

Some states require prospective teachers to have masters' degrees in education and specialized technology training to keep them familiar with more modern teaching methods using computers and the Internet.

Certification or Licensing

Public school teachers must be licensed under regulations established by the state in which they are teaching. If moving, teachers have to comply with any other regulations in their new state to be able to teach, though many states have reciprocity agreements that make it easier for teachers to change locations.

Licensure examinations test prospective teachers for competency in basic subjects such as mathematics, reading, writing, teaching, and other subject matter proficiency. In addition, many states are moving towards a performance-based evaluation for licensing. In this case, after passing the teaching examination, prospective teachers are given provisional licenses. Only after proving themselves capable in the classroom are they eligible for a full license.

Another growing trend spurred by recent teacher shortages is alternative licensure arrangements. For those who have a bachelor's degree but lack formal education courses and training in the classroom, states can issue a provisional license. These workers immediately begin teaching under the supervision of a licensed educator for one to two years and take education classes outside of their working hours. Once they have completed the required coursework and gained experience in the classroom, they are granted a full license. This flexible licensing arrangement has helped to bring additional teachers into school systems needing instructors.

Other Requirements

Many consider the desire to teach a calling. This calling is based on a love of children and a dedication to their welfare. If you want to become a teacher, you must respect children as individuals, with personalities, strengths, and weaknesses of their own. You must also be patient and self-disciplined to manage a large group independently. Teachers make a powerful impression on children, so they need to serve as good role models. "Treat students with kindness and understanding, rules and consequences," Andrea LoCastro suggests. "Be nice, yet strict. They'll love you for it."

Exploring

To explore the teaching career, look for leadership opportunities that involve working with children. You might find summer work as a counselor in a summer camp, as a leader of a scout troop, or as an assistant in a public park or community center. Look for opportunities to tutor younger students or coach children's athletic teams. Local community theaters may need directors and assistants for summer children's productions. Day care centers often hire high school students for late afternoon and weekend work.

Employers

According to the U.S. Department of Labor, there are 1.4 million kindergarten and elementary school teachers employed in the United States. Teachers are needed at public and private schools, including parochial schools, Montessori schools, and day care centers that offer full-day elementary programs. Teachers are also hired by charter schools, which are smaller, deregulated schools that receive public funding. Although rural areas maintain schools, more teaching positions are available in urban or suburban areas.

Starting Out

After obtaining a college degree and completing the teacher certification process, including the student teaching requirement, prospective teachers have many avenues for finding a job. College placement offices and state departments of education maintain listings of job openings. Many local schools advertise teaching positions in newspapers. Another option is directly contacting the administration in the schools in which you'd like to work. While looking for a full-time position, you can work as a substitute teacher. In more urban areas with many schools, you may be able to find full-time substitute work.

Advancement

As teachers acquire experience or additional education, they can expect higher wages and more responsibilities. Teachers with leadership skills and an interest in administrative work may advance to serve as principals or supervisors, though the number of these positions is limited and competition is fierce. Others may advance to work as *senior* or *mentor teachers* who assist less experienced staff. Another move may be into higher education, teaching education classes at a college or university. For most of these positions, additional education is required.

Other common career transitions are into related fields. With additional preparation, teachers can become librarians, reading specialists, or counselors.

"I intend to continue teaching as my career," says Andrea LoCastro. "I am not at all interested in moving up to administration. I will, however, pursue a master's in teaching after receiving tenure."

Earnings

According to the U.S. Department of Labor, the median annual salary for kindergarten, elementary, and secondary school teachers was between $33,590 to $37,890 in 1998. The lowest 10 percent earned between $19,710 and $24,390; the highest 10 percent earned between $53,720 and $70,030.

In 1999, the American Federation of Teachers reported that the average salary for beginning teachers with a bachelor's degree was $26,639. The average maximum salary paid to teachers with master's degrees was $47,439.

Teachers often supplement their earnings through teaching summer classes, coaching sports, sponsoring a club, or other extracurricular work. In 1999, over half of all teachers belonged to unions such as the American Federation of Teachers or the National Education Association. These unions bargain with schools over contract conditions such as wages, hours, and benefits. Depending on the state, teachers usually receive a retirement plan, sick leave, and health and life insurance. Some systems grant teachers sabbatical leave.

Work Environment

Most teachers are contracted to work 10 months out of the year, with a two-month vacation during the summer. During their summer break, many continue their education to renew or upgrade their teaching licenses and earn higher salaries. Teachers in schools that operate year-round work eight-week sessions with one-week breaks in between and a five-week vacation in the winter.

Teachers work in generally pleasant conditions, although some older schools may have poor heating or electrical systems. The work can seem confining, requiring them to remain in the classroom throughout most of the day. Although the job is not overly strenuous, dealing with busy children all day can be tiring and trying. Teachers must stand for many hours each day, do a lot of talking, show energy and enthusiasm, and may have to handle discipline problems. But, according to Andrea LoCastro, problems with students are usually overshadowed by their successes. "Just knowing a child is learning something because of you is the most rewarding feeling, especially when you and the child have struggled together to understand it."

Outlook

According to the *Occupational Outlook Handbook,* employment opportunities for teachers (grades K-12) are expected to grow as fast as the average for all occupations through 2008. The need to replace retiring teachers will provide many opportunities nationwide.

The demand for teachers varies widely depending on geographic area. Inner-city schools characterized by poor working conditions and low salaries often suffer a shortage of teachers. In addition, more opportunities exist for those who specialize in a subject in which it is harder to attract qualified teachers, such as mathematics, science, or foreign languages.

The U.S. Department of Education predicts that 1 million new teachers will be needed by 2008 to meet rising enrollments and replace the large number of retiring teachers. The National Education Association believes this will be a difficult challenge to meet because of low teacher salaries. Higher salaries along with other necessary changes, such as smaller classroom sizes and safer schools, will be necessary to attract new teachers and retain experienced ones. Other challenges for the profession involve attracting more men into teaching. The percentage of male teachers continues to decline.

In order to improve education, drastic changes are being considered by some districts. Some private companies are managing public schools in the hope of providing better facilities, faculty, and equipment. Teacher organizations are concerned about taking school management away from communities and turning it over to remote corporate headquarters.

Charter schools and voucher programs are two other controversial alternatives to traditional public education. Publicly funded charter schools are not guided by the rules and regulations of traditional public schools. Some view these schools as places of innovation and improved educational methods; others see them as ill-equipped and unfairly funded with money that could better benefit local school districts. Vouchers, which exist only in a few cities, use public tax dollars to allow students to attend private schools. In theory, the vouchers allow for more choices in education for poor and minority students. Teacher organizations see some danger in giving public funds to unregulated private schools.

For More Information

For information about careers, union membership, and issues affecting teachers, contact the following organizations:

American Federation of Teachers
555 New Jersey Avenue, NW
Washington, DC 20001
Tel: 202-879-4400
Email: online@aft.org
Web: http://www.aft.org

National Education Association
1201 16th Street, NW
Washington, DC 20036
Tel: 202-833-4000
Web: http://www.nea.org

ESL Teachers

School Subjects
English
Social studies

Personal Skills
Communication/ideas
Helping/teaching

Minimum Education Level
Bachelor's degree

Salary Range
$25,000 to $39,000 to $47,000

Certification or Licensing
Required by all states

Outlook
About as fast as the average

Overview

English as Second Language (ESL) teachers specialize in teaching people of all ages the English language. Most students are immigrants and refugees, while some may be children of foreign-born parents, or children who may be living in a home where English is not spoken as the primary language.

History

Less than four centuries ago, no more than a few million people spoke English. Today, it is the primary language of about a third of a billion people, and is spoken as a second language by tens of millions of others. English is considered necessary to conduct international business, and people everywhere choose to speak English in order to communicate with many people. However, English is considered one of the most difficult languages to learn, primarily because of its many irregularities. It has a larger vocabulary than any other language and incorporates numerous slang terms and newly coined words and phrases.

While English has been taught in the American school systems for decades, ESL instructors have emerged as a result of increased immigrants and refugees, as well as a growing number of children born to non-English speaking parents.

According to a report by the U.S. Bureau of the Census, the estimated foreign-born population of the United States in March 1997 was 25.8 million. This is a 30 percent increase over the 1990 census figure and was the largest foreign-born population reported in U.S. history. This trend is likely to continue, which will only increase the demand for ESL teachers. According to the National Center for Education Statistics, the demand for placement in ESL classes has grown and there is a long waiting list for ESL classes in many parts of the country.

The Job

Today, many public and private schools employ teachers trained as ESL instructors. ESL teachers do not usually speak the language of the students they teach. However, many teachers try to learn some key words and phrases in their students' native tongues in order to communicate better. ESL teachers teach English usage and pronunciation, as well as core language skills necessary for students to participate in other classes such as math and science, and in order to interact socially with other students. According to Linda Lahann, an ESL instructor in Iowa with 19 years of experience, the students she teaches often do not have a good background in reading in their own language. In some countries, reading skills are not encouraged. "Not having this good base makes it even more difficult to learn the language in a new country," says Lahann.

The primary goal of ESL teachers is to help students learn to use the English language to communicate both verbally and in writing. They also try to build students' confidence through instruction and interaction. It is important to encourage students to become involved in social activities. Lahann says that it is very rewarding to watch her students participate in extracurricular activities and see them embrace the English language and American culture.

Classroom methods may include games, videos, computers, field trips, role-playing, and other activities to make learning fun and interesting for students. Classes often center on teaching conversation skills, telephone skills, the art of listening, and the idioms of the English language. The instructor helps the students learn correct pronunciation, sentence structure, communication skills, and vocabulary.

As any other teacher, ESL teachers prepare lesson plans and exams, keep student records, and fulfill other assignments as required by the school system. They keep current in the field by reading books and researching new teaching methods. Many states require teachers to take college-level courses to maintain their teaching certificates.

ESL teachers may work with immigrants or refugees, or perhaps children of parents who may have immigrated and not learned the English language. In some homes, English is not spoken as the primary language, making it difficult for the child to relate to peers and teachers when entering school. Those who teach in border states will be more likely to teach immigrant students. If you teach in other states, you may be teaching refugees who have witnessed the tragedies of war.

"Not only do I deal with language," says Lahann, "but I must also deal with the students' emotions and their experiences with culture shock. Many of these refugees have seen and experienced war." Lahann, who has taught students from 21 different countries, says that there are many different levels of understanding that her students go through. She says for some students, it may take three to five years of ESL classes until they reach the point where they can compete academically. "The most special thing, though," says Lahann, "is watching the light bulb come on. Ah ha! You see that they have finally broken the code. That makes it all worthwhile."

Many ESL teachers teach adults in adult basic education programs. With the increase of refugees and immigrants to the United States, community centers, libraries, churches, and assistance centers are offering ESL classes as well. Some immigration and refugee assistance centers and organizations may offer classes in learning the English language as part of their programs.

Teaching the adult learner often requires teaching skills that are different than those required to teach young people. Frequently, adults are not comfortable being back in a learning environment, so teachers may have to help them develop study habits and regain their confidence in the classroom. In addition, many adult students have jobs and may have families to care for, so teachers must be aware of the other commitments students might have and be able to adjust their teaching methods and expectations.

ESL instructors might be hired by a company to provide instruction to its workers as a part of the company's employee training or employee assistance programs, or simply as a courtesy to its workers. Classes might be held during break or lunch, after work hours, or the class may be a required part of the employee's workday.

Simply because of the nature of the job, ESL teachers may get emotionally involved with their students. "I am often invited to participate in cultural celebrations in the community as well as family events such as weddings," says Lahann. "This is exciting and rewarding to be a part of their social and family life as well."

Many communities have a strong networking system that involves churches, schools, health providers, resettlement programs, and other groups. ESL instructors may get involved with these groups and make visits to the students' homes to meet their families. They sometimes work with translators to communicate with the families and students. Some school systems and community programs also use translators to help the families communicate with medical providers, social workers, and government officials.

ESL instructors also find many opportunities overseas teaching English as a foreign language (EFL).

Requirements

High School

For ESL teachers courses in English, foreign language, and social studies are highly recommended. Joining a foreign language club is suggested. Becoming a foreign exchange student or housing a foreign exchange student can also be a valuable experience if you are considering this career. Participate in community multicultural events and volunteer with community relocation centers. Many churches also have refugee assistance programs that can offer excellent exposure to helping people from other countries.

Postsecondary Training

Teaching certificate requirements vary by state. There are about 500 accredited teacher education programs in the United States and most are designed to meet the requirements of the state in which they are located. The National Council for Accreditation of Teacher Education, listed under the For More Information section of this article, can provide information on teacher education programs. Some states may require that you pass a test before being admitted to an education program.

While a college major in ESL is fairly new, there are some programs that do offer it. If offered, you may choose to major in ESL, or you may major in education with a concentration in ESL as a subject area. Student teaching is almost always required in a teaching program. You will be placed in a school to work with a full-time teacher. You will observe the class, learn how to prepare lesson plans, and actually work with students and other teachers.

Besides licensure and courses in education, prospective teachers at the secondary level usually need 24 to 36 hours of college work in ESL-related classes. Some states may require a master's degree.

ESL teachers of adult students do not need an education degree or a license. There are a variety of training programs available for ESL teachers of adults. These programs usually last from four to 12 weeks and upon successful completion, a diploma or certificate is awarded.

Certification or Licensing

Teachers in public schools must be licensed under regulations established by the Department of Education of the state in which they teach. Not all states require licensure for teachers in private or parochial schools.

If you are pursuing a career as an ESL teacher, you should check the specific requirements of the state where you plan to teach. According to the National Clearinghouse for Bilingual Education, the results of a 1999 survey of State Education Agencies reported that 37 states and the District of Columbia offer ESL teacher certification or endorsement. In addition to offering teacher certification in ESL, 23 states require that teachers placed in ESL classrooms must be certified in ESL.

In some states you may be required to complete continuing education courses in order to maintain your teaching certificate.

Overseas employers of ESL teachers may require a certificate and experience.

Other Requirements

ESL teachers must be patient and have the ability to relate to people of other nationalities and cultures. You should have an interest in other cultures and in the history and traditions of other countries and nationalities. An ability to relate to people from all walks of life is also necessary to be successful as an ESL teacher.

If you plan to teach adults, you should be aware of the different ways people absorb information and be able to adapt your teaching skills to successfully teach older students.

Exploring

Get involved with people of different cultures through community service, school activities, or church programs. If possible, travel to other countries and learn first-hand about other cultures. Speak to ESL teachers about their teaching methods and how they adjust their teaching approach to reach students who have limited English language skills. Volunteer to help with any assistance, relocation, or referral programs that your community or church might have for immigrants or refugees.

Employers

Teachers are needed at public and private schools, including parochial schools and vocational schools. Depending on the size of the school, its geographic location, and the number of students in need of assistance, some schools may hire teachers primarily as ESL instructors. Others may hire you to teach other subjects along with ESL classes. Larger cities and areas of refugee relocation and large immigrant populations will probably provide you with the most job opportunities.

Some community-based and government assistance programs may hire ESL teachers. Many adult education teachers are self-employed and work on a contract basis for industries, community and junior colleges, universities, community organizations, job training centers, and religious organizations. Relocation services might also hire ESL teachers on a contract or part-time basis.

Overseas employers hire ESL teachers, usually for short-term assignments. Many people become ESL teachers because it allows them to earn a living while seeing the world and experiencing other cultures.

Starting Out

After completing the required certification program for the state in which you want to teach, you can work with your college placement office to find a teaching position. The departments of education in your state may have a listing of job openings. Most major newspapers list available teaching positions in their classified ad sections. Teaching organizations such as the

National Education Association and the American Federation of Teachers also list teaching positions. You may also apply directly to the principals or superintendents of the schools in which you'd like to teach. Substitute teaching can provide experience as well as possible job contacts.

Contacting schools or community assistance programs, as well as adult education programs, may provide some job opportunities. Your college professors might have job hunting suggestions as well as names of people who might be able to assist you.

Advancement

Advancement opportunities into educational administrative positions or corporate or government training positions may be available for those instructors with advanced degrees.

Lateral moves are also common in school systems. For instance, an ESL teacher may transfer to a position as a counselor or choose to teach another subject. Other opportunities may be available within community and government-based programs that assist refugees and immigrants.

Earnings

While there are no specific salary reports for ESL teachers, the American Federation of Teachers reported that the U.S. average salary for teachers in a 1999 salary survey was $39,347. The average salary for a beginning teacher with a bachelor's degree was $26,639. The average maximum salary for a teacher with a master's degree was $47,439. The Bureau of Labor Statistics reported that most K-12 teachers earn between $34,000 and $38,000.

Most teachers join the American Federation of Teachers or the National Education Association. These unions bargain on behalf of the teachers regarding contract conditions such as wages, hours, and benefits. Depending on the state, teachers usually receive a retirement plan, sick leave, and health and life insurance. Some schools may grant you sabbatical leave.

Overseas employers usually offer low pay, but they sometimes offer housing, airfare, medical care, or other benefits as part of the teaching contract.

Work Environment

Many ESL teachers work in primary and secondary classrooms. While the job is not overly strenuous, it can be tiring and trying. Some school environments can be tense if drugs, gangs, and other problems are present. Although there has been increased media coverage of school violence, reports indicate that it has actually decreased over the years.

Most traditional classroom teachers work a typical school day but you can also expect to put in extra hours preparing for classes and meeting other teaching duty requirements. If your other duties require sponsorship of clubs or coaching, you may have to work some nights or weekends. You may also be required to be at the school extra hours to accommodate parents and students who may want to meet with you.

If you choose to teach adult education classes or other community-based classes you may be required to hold classes at night to accommodate your students' work and family schedules. ESL teachers who primarily teach adults may hold classes in corporate classrooms, libraries, or meeting rooms as well as local colleges or schools. The physical teaching conditions and locations can vary.

Just as there is a large demand for ESL instructors in the United States, there is also a need for ESL educators overseas. Many teachers with these skills may find opportunities to teach in classrooms in foreign countries or on military bases overseas. If you instruct overseas you may teach in a traditional classroom environment, or you may be required to perform in less than desirable settings depending on the culture and the economics of the area.

Outlook

The U.S. Department of Education predicts that one million new teachers will be needed by 2008 to meet rising enrollments and to replace the large number of retiring teachers.

If you specialize in ESL you should have a promising future in the American school system. According to a 1998 salary survey conducted by the American Federation of Teachers, school districts reported that there was a considerable shortage of teachers of bilingual education. Similarly, in a report by the U.S. Department of Education, 27.2 percent of U.S. schools reported in a 1993-94 survey that they had bilingual/ESL vacancies that they found difficult or impossible to fill. This situation is expected to continue.

The Bureau of Labor Statistics reports that the demand for adult education teachers is expected to grow as fast as the average for all occupations through 2008.

The increased immigrant and refugee populations in the United States will also increase the need for instruction in the English language, whether in the school system, the community, or the workplace. Many community and social service agencies, as well as community colleges, are offering assistance to immigrants and refugees and will need the services of ESL teachers.

For More Information

For information on teaching careers and accredited education programs, contact the following organizations:

American Federation of Teachers
555 New Jersey Avenue, NW
Washington, DC 20001
Tel: 202-879-4400
Email: online@aft.org
Web: http://www.aft.org

National Council for Accreditation of Teacher Education
2010 Massachusetts Avenue, NW
Washington, DC 20036-1023
Tel: 202-466-7496
Email: ncate@ncate.org
Web: http://www.ncate.org

For information on ESL teaching careers, contact the following organizations:

National Education Association
1201 16th Street, NW
Washington, DC 20036
Tel: 202-833-4000
Web: http://www.nea.org

Teachers of English to Speakers of Other Languages, Inc.
700 South Washington Street, Suite 200
Alexandria, VA 22314
Tel: 703-836-0774
Email: info@tesol.org
Web: http://www.tesol.edu

Guidance Counselors

English Psychology	School Subjects
Helping/teaching Leadership/management	Personal Skills
Primarily indoors Primarily one location	Work Environment
Master's degree	Minimum Education Level
$20,000 to $38,650 to $74,000	Salary Range
Required by all states	Certification or Licensing
Faster than the average	Outlook

Overview

Guidance counselors provide a planned program of guidance services for all students, principally in junior and senior high schools. In addition to helping students plan for college and careers, guidance counselors listen to students' problems, advise students, and help them develop coping skills and learn to become good problem-solvers and decision-makers on their own.

Although guidance counselors often meet with students individually, they may also work with groups, organizing several students for special meetings to address a problem or issue that the students have in common.

History

Counseling in secondary schools, as a comprehensive guidance service, is an outgrowth of the earlier program of vocational guidance in schools. Such programs were slowly adopted by school systems through the 1920s with Boston and New York being among the first, but during the Depression years, school budgets were at a low point and the vocational guidance movement came to a standstill.

After World War II, guidance services began to show signs of growth. Many factors contributed to the sudden spurt. There was a great migration from rural to urban living, and city schools became overcrowded. Students lost their individual identity in the crowds of fellow students. More courses were being offered in more schools, and choices were difficult to make. Changes in careers because of technological developments made it difficult for parents to help their children with wise career choices. Living standards improved, and more parents, who themselves had not gone to college, planned a college education for their children. In the years following World War II, school guidance programs grew both in number and in expanded fields. Many colleges and universities initiated training programs for guidance counselors, and licensure standards for counselors were established or upgraded. The U.S. Office of Education embarked upon an ambitious leadership program for guidance services as the need for professionals in the field increased.

The Job

Guidance counselors work in a school setting to provide a planned program of guidance services for the benefit of all students enrolled in the school. The guidance program is not one single plan, but is the combination of many related activities. It has several aims, but its most important one is to help each student in the process of growth toward maturity. The guidance program is designed to help students achieve independence.

All guidance programs are unique. Each one is built especially for the school in which it functions. Guidance counselors confer with parents, with such professional personnel as school psychologists, social workers, and health officers, and with other faculty and staff members to assure a totally effective school program. They meet with students on an appointment, walk-in, or teacher referral basis to talk about students' personal problems or concerns; to review academic, attendance, or conduct records; or to discuss anything else that may be an issue to the students, faculty, or parents.

Jim Buist is a middle school counselor. "I work with about 800 young people during a highly charged transitional period of their lives," he says. "My primary role as a school counselor is to aid these young people in a successful educational process." This involves a number of tasks: scheduling (matching students with teachers and courses); testing (to monitor progress); and counseling (to guide young people through the troubles of adolescence).

Students seek out Buist's advice on such subjects as family issues, peer pressure, alcohol/drug problems, the development of romantic relationships, and illness and death. "Besides working with the students themselves," Buist says, "I have the obligation and opportunity to work with other professionals as teams or supports, as well as with parents who are often looking for the manual that was supposed to come with their children."

In addition to dealing directly with students, guidance counselors collect and organize materials for students to read about such topics as peer-pressure, self-esteem, occupations, and post-high school educational opportunities. They conduct group guidance meetings in which topics of special concern or interest to the age-group involved are discussed. For example, they may direct an orientation program for students new to the school. In addition, they organize, administer, score, and interpret the school's standardized testing program.

Guidance counselors assist students in choosing their course of studies, developing more effective study habits, and making tentative choices regarding goals for the future. They help students in selecting the post-high school training that will best meet their educational and vocational needs. They also assist students in applying for admission to colleges or vocational schools, help locate scholarships, and write reference letters to college admissions officers or prospective employers.

Guidance counselors plan, organize, and conduct events such as career days and college days. They may conduct follow-up studies of students who have left school or graduated, requesting their help in evaluating the curriculum in the light of their post-high school work experiences.

Guidance counselors also conduct in-service education courses for other faculty members or speak at meetings of interested members of the community. They refer students with problems that are beyond the scope of the school to address, to such community resources as social welfare agencies, child guidance clinics, health departments, or other services.

Requirements

High School

Enroll in a college-preparatory curriculum to prepare for the college degrees required of guidance counselors. You should take courses in humanities, social studies, psychology, and speech. Courses in mathematics are important, because mathematical and statistical theory underlie much of the standardized testing program. You should take English courses because both written and spoken communication with students, parents, and administrators are important components to this occupation.

Postsecondary Training

The basic requirement for a school counselor in many states is a bachelor's degree and certain stipulated courses at the graduate level. As an undergraduate, you'll probably major in education so that you'll have the course work necessary for teacher certification. Certification is a requirement for working as a guidance counselors in most states. About six in 10 counselors hold master's degrees. The American Counseling Association provides information to students when selecting graduate programs in counselor education. To get accepted into a graduate program, you'll have to have a bachelor's degree, and possibly a teaching certificate, and a few years teaching experience. These programs usually require at least two years of additional study, as well as an internship. Course subjects include career development, group counseling, substance abuse counseling, art therapy, and grief and loss counseling.

Certification or Licensing

You must be certified by your state to work as a counselor; the requirements for certification vary from state to state. Most state licensure standards require that counselors have teaching experience. This experience may be as short as one year or as long as two to three. Some states also require that counselors have work experience outside of the teaching field.

Other Requirements

Your most important asset will be your ability to relate easily and well to others. To achieve a sound relationship with other adults and with children, you must have a sincere interest in other people and their welfare. You must be able to relate to all kinds of people and situations, and to be sensitive to issues of race, religion, sexual orientation, and disability. Jim Buist lists empathy, patience, and listening skills among the personal qualities that make a good counselor. He emphasizes that counselors should have some teaching experience in their background. Without that experience, Buist says, "you'll be missing the experience that you'll need day in and day out. It would be difficult, if not impossible, to learn these skills 'on the job.'"

Exploring

Your best resource for information about work as a guidance counselor is right in your own high school. Ask your school's counselor how he or she got started in the career, and about the nature of the job. You may even be allowed to assist your counselor with a variety of projects, like career days, or college recruitment. With your counselor's help, you can identify some of the particular issues affecting your fellow students, and come up with ways to address the issues with special projects. You can also get a sense of a counselor's job by working on the school newspaper. As a reporter, you'll have the opportunity to interview students, get to know their concerns, and write editorials about these issues.

The American Counseling Association publishes a great deal of information about the field, both online through their Web site (www.counseling.org) and in their monthly newspaper, *Counseling Today.*

Employers

Counselors are employed in elementary, middle, and high schools all across the country. They work in both public and private schools. Though counselors are considered important to a school system, not every school has its own counselor on staff. Some counselors have offices in more than one school; for example, they may work for both a middle school and a high school, or they may work for other schools in the district.

Starting Out

While some students do enroll in master's programs right after finishing their undergraduate programs, most experts advise the aspiring guidance counselor to have at least a few years of teaching experience under their belt before they pursue a master's degree in counselor education. Some people work for several years as teachers before considering a degree in school counseling. College professors and advisers should be able to direct recent graduates to sources of counseling positions. Some state boards of education maintain job lines, as do many public school districts. These jobs are also advertised in the newspaper.

The American Counseling Association lists job openings in its publication, *Counseling Today,* and on their Web site. The American School Counselor Association offers professional development programs to help members expand skills, knowledge, and networking opportunities.

Advancement

Schools with more than one counselor on the staff offer the opportunity for staff members to advance to *school guidance director.* The title may be misleading, however, as one does not usually "direct" the program; rather, one coordinates it. The school principal is usually the actual director of the program. Most advancement within the guidance counselor position will be in the form of wage increases.

Some counselors with many years of experience may be appointed as *guidance coordinator* or *school system director.* Their duties usually include program development.

For the most part, counselors are promoted to positions outside of counseling itself, such as to administration or supervisory jobs. Some counselors obtain advanced degrees and become college or university teachers. Jim Buist has had many opportunities to move into administrative positions, but has turned them down. "I know I would miss the contact with the students, parents, and teachers," he says.

Earnings

Wages for guidance counselors vary by region of the country, school and district size, and age of the students. Larger districts typically offer higher salaries, and counselors working with high school students tend to earn more than counselors for younger grades. The lowest salaries for guidance counselors in the United States are in the Southeast, and the highest are on the West Coast. Beginning salaries in the field average about $20,000, while the most experienced counselor can earn over $74,000. According to the

Occupational Outlook Handbook, the average salary for school counselors was $38,650 a year in 1998.

Because guidance counselors work on an academic calendar, they typically get a good amount of vacation time, especially in the summer. Some counselors use this time to take further university courses. Counselors receive the benefits and pension plans provided by the school or district for which they work.

Work Environment

Most guidance counselors have a private office in which to talk with students, parents, and faculty members. But they also work in other parts of the school, leading presentations, coordinating events, and speaking to classes of students. Counselors find it rewarding to help students through their problems, and to help them plan for their futures, but they also have the stress of guiding young people through difficult times. "This is an age where a counselor/teacher can make a difference," Jim Buist says.

Guidance counselors usually work more than 40 hours a week, spending a part of each day in conferences and meetings. They often arrive at school earlier than do many other staff members and may return in the evening to talk with parents who are unable to come to the school during working hours.

Outlook

Though violence in the schools has been decreasing, the number of students afraid to go to school has increased. This increase is likely a result of the rash of shootings and gang-related warfare that plagued some schools in the late 1990s. The federal government has called for more counselors in the schools to help address issues of violence and other dangers, such as drug use. The government, along with counseling professionals, is also working to remove the stigma of mental illness, and to encourage more children and families to seek help from school counselors. To keep schools safe, guidance counselors may be more actively involved in instituting and maintaining discipline policies.

Technology will continue to assist counselors in their jobs. With Internet access in the libraries, counselors can easily direct students to specific career information, scholarship applications, and college Web sites. School counselors may also follow the lead of Internet counselors and offer guidance online; students seeking anonymity can request information and advice from their counselors through email and other online services.

For More Information

For information about current issues in counseling and graduate school programs, contact:

American Counseling Association
5999 Stevenson Avenue
Alexandria, VA 22304
Tel: 800-347-6647
Web: http://www.counseling.org

For information about membership, publications, and professional development programs, contact:

American School Counselor Association
801 North Fairfax Street, Suite 310
Alexandria, VA 22314
Tel: 800-306-4722
Web: http://www.schoolcounselor.org

Interpreters and Translators

English Foreign language	School Subjects
Communication/ideas Helping/teaching	Personal Skills
Primarily indoors Primarily multiple locations	Work Environment
Bachelor's degree	Minimum Education Level
$22,000 to $30,000 to $80,000	Salary Range
Recommended	Certification or Licensing
About as fast as the average	Outlook

Overview

An *interpreter* translates spoken passages of a foreign language into another specified language. The job is often designated by the language interpreted, such as Spanish or Japanese. In addition, many interpreters specialize according to subject matter. For example, *medical interpreters* have extensive knowledge of and experience in the health care field, while *court* or *judiciary interpreters* speak both a second language and the "language" of law. *Interpreters for the deaf* aid in the communication between people who are unable to hear and those who can.

In contrast to interpreters, *translators* focus on written materials, such as books, plays, technical or scientific papers, legal documents, laws, treaties, and decrees. A *sight translator* performs a combination of interpreting and translating by reading printed material in one language while reciting it aloud in another. In the United States, approximately 1,000 interpreters and 2,000 translators currently work full-time.

History

Until recently, most people who spoke two languages well enough to interpret and translate did so only on the side, working full-time in some other occupation. For example, many diplomats and high-level government officials employed people who were able to serve as interpreters and translators, but only as needed. These employees spent the rest of their time assisting in other ways.

Interpreting and translating as full-time professions have emerged only recently, partly in response to the need for high-speed communication across the globe. The increasing use of complex diplomacy also demanded full-time translating and interpreting professionals. For many years, diplomacy was practiced largely between two nations at a time. Rarely did conferences involve more than two languages at one time. The League of Nations, established by the Treaty of Versailles in 1919, established a new pattern of communication. Although the "language of diplomacy" was then considered to be French, diplomatic discussions were carried out in many different languages for the first time.

Since the early 1920s, multinational conferences have become commonplace. Trade and educational conferences are now held with participants of many nations in attendance. Responsible for international diplomacy after the League of Nations dissolved, the United Nations now employs many full-time interpreters and translators, providing career opportunities for qualified people. In addition, the European Common Market (headquartered in Brussels, Belgium) employs a large number of interpreters.

The Job

Although interpreters are needed for a variety of languages for different venues and circumstances, there are only two basic systems of interpretation—simultaneous and consecutive. Spurred in part by the invention and development of electronic sound equipment, simultaneous interpretation has been in use since the charter of the United Nations.

Simultaneous interpreters are able to convert a spoken sentence instantaneously. Some are so skilled that they are able to complete a sentence in the second language at almost the precise moment that the speaker is conversing in the original language. Such interpreters are usually familiar with the speaking habits of the speaker to be able to anticipate the way in which the sentence will be completed. The interpreter may also make judgments about the intent of the sentence or phrase from the speaker's gestures, facial expressions, and inflections. While working at a fast pace, the interpreter must be careful not to summarize, edit, or in any way change the meaning of what is being said.

In contrast, *consecutive interpreters* wait until the speaker has paused to convert speech into a second language. In this case, the speaker waits until the interpreter has finished before resuming the speech. Since every sentence is repeated in consecutive interpretation, this method takes longer than simultaneous interpretation.

For both systems, interpreters are placed so that they can clearly see and hear all that is taking place. In formal situations, such as those at the United Nations (UN) and other international conferences, interpreters are often assigned to a glass-enclosed booth. Speeches are transmitted to the booth, and interpreters, in turn, translate the speaker's words into a microphone. Each UN delegate can tune in the voice of the appropriate interpreter. Because of the difficulty of the job, these simultaneous interpreters usually work in pairs, each working 30-minute shifts.

All *international conference interpreters* are simultaneous interpreters. Many interpreters, however, work in situations other than formal diplomatic meetings. For example, interpreters are needed for negotiations of all kinds, as well as for legal, financial, medical, and business purposes. Court or judiciary interpreters, for example, work in courtrooms and at attorney-client meetings, depositions, and witness preparation sessions.

Other interpreters serve on-call, traveling with visitors from foreign countries who are touring the United States. Usually, these language specialists use consecutive interpretation. Their job is to make sure that whatever the visitors say is understood and that they also understand what is being said to them. Still other interpreters accompany groups of U.S. citizens on official tours abroad. On such assignments, they may be sent to any foreign country and might be away from the United States for long periods of time.

Interpreters also work on short-term assignments. Services may be required for only brief intervals, such as for a special conference or single interview with press representatives.

While interpreters focus on the spoken word, translators work with written language. They read and translate novels, plays, essays, nonfiction and technical works, legal documents, records and reports, speeches, and other written material. Translators generally follow a certain set of procedures in their work. They begin by reading the text, taking careful notes on what they do not understand. To translate questionable passages, they look up words and terms in specialized dictionaries and glossaries. They may also do additional reading on the subject to arrive at a better understanding. Finally, they write translated drafts in the target language.

Requirements

High School

High school students interested in becoming interpreters or translators should take a variety of English courses, because most translate a foreign language into English. The study of one or more foreign languages is vital. If you are interested in becoming proficient in one or more of the Romance languages, such as Italian, French, or Spanish, basic courses in Latin will prove to be valuable.

While you should devote as much time as possible to the study of at least one foreign language, other helpful courses include speech, business, cultural studies, humanities, world history, geography, and political science. In fact, any course that emphasizes the written and/or spoken word will be valuable to aspiring interpreters or translators. In addition, knowledge of a particular subject matter in which you may have interest, such as health, law, or science, will give you a professional edge if you want to specialize. Finally, courses in typing and word processing are recommended, especially if you want to pursue a career as a translator.

Postsecondary Training

Because interpreters and translators need to be proficient in grammar, have an excellent vocabulary in the chosen language, and have sound knowledge in a wide variety of subjects, employers generally require applicants have at least a college degree. Scientific and professional interpreters are best qualified if they have graduate degrees.

In addition to language and field-specialty skills, you should take college courses that will allow you to develop effective techniques in public speaking, particularly if you're planning to pursue a career as an interpreter. Courses such as speech and debate will improve your diction and confidence as a public speaker.

Hundreds of colleges and universities in the United States offer degrees in languages. In addition, educational institutions now provide programs and degrees specialized for interpreting and translating. Georgetown University offers both undergraduate and graduate programs in linguistics. The Translation Studies Program at the University of Texas at Brownsville allows students to earn certificates in translation studies at the undergraduate level. Graduate degrees in interpretation and translation may be earned at the University of California at Santa Barbara, the University of Puerto Rico, and the Monterey Institute of International Studies. Many of these programs include both general and specialized courses, such as medical interpretation and legal translation.

Academic programs for the training of interpreters can be found in Europe as well. The University of Geneva's Interpreters' School is highly regarded among professionals in the field.

Certification or Licensing

Although interpreters and translators need not be certified to obtain jobs, employers often show preference to certified applicants. Court interpreters who successfully pass a strict written test may earn certification from the Administrative Office of the United States Courts. Interpreters for the deaf who pass an examination may qualify for either comprehensive or legal certification by the Registry of Interpreters for the Deaf. Foreign language translators may be granted accreditation by the American Translators Association (ATA) upon successful completion of required exams. ATA accreditation is available for the following languages: Arabic, Chinese, Dutch, Finnish, French, German, Hungarian, Italian, Japanese, Polish, Portuguese, Russian, and Spanish.

The U.S. Department of State has specific test requirements for its translators and interpreters. Applicants must have several years of foreign language practice, advanced education in the language (preferably abroad), and be fluent in vocabulary for a very broad range of subjects.

Other Requirements

Interpreters should be able to speak at least two languages fluently, without strong accents. They should be knowledgeable of not only the foreign language but also of the culture and social norms of the region or country in which it is spoken. Both interpreters and translators should read daily newspapers in the languages in which they work to keep current in both developments and usage.

Interpreters must have good hearing, a sharp mind, and a strong, clear, and pleasant voice. They must be able to be precise and quick in their translation. In addition to being flexible and versatile in their work, both interpreters and translators should have self-discipline and patience. Above all, they should have an interest in and love of language.

Finally, interpreters must be honest and trustworthy, observing any existing codes of confidentiality at all times. The ethical code of interpreters and translators is a rigid one. They must hold private proceedings in strict confidence. Ethics also demands that interpreters and translators not distort the meaning of the sentences that are spoken or written. No matter how much they may agree or disagree with the speaker or writer, interpreters and translators must be objective in their work. In addition, information they obtain in the process of interpretation or translation must never be passed along to unauthorized groups or people.

Exploring

If you have an opportunity to visit the United Nations, you can watch the proceedings to get some idea of the techniques and responsibilities of the job of the interpreter. Occasionally, an international conference session is televised, and the work of the interpreters can be observed. You should note, however, that interpreters who work at these conferences are in the top positions of the vocation. Not everyone may aspire to such jobs. The work of interpreters and translators is usually less public, but not necessarily less interesting.

If you have adequate skills in a foreign language, you might consider traveling in a country in which the language is spoken. If you can converse easily and without a strong accent and can interpret to others who may not understand the language well, you may have what it takes to work as an interpreter or translator.

For any international field, it is important that you familiarize yourself with other cultures. You can even arrange to regularly correspond with a pen pal in a foreign country. You may also want to join a school club that focuses on a particular language, such as the French Club or the Spanish Club. If no such clubs exist, consider forming one. Student clubs can allow you to hone your foreign language speaking and writing skills and learn about other cultures.

Finally, participating on a speech or debate team can allow you to practice your public speaking skills, increase your confidence, and polish your overall appearance by working on eye contact, gestures, facial expressions, tone, and other elements used in public speaking.

Employers

There are approximately 1,000 interpreters and 2,000 translators working full-time in the United States. Although many interpreters and translators work for government or international agencies, some are employed by private firms. Large import-export companies often have interpreters or translators on their payrolls, although these employees generally perform additional duties for the firm. International banks, companies, organizations, and associations often employ both interpreters and translators to facilitate communication. In addition, translators and interpreters work at publishing houses, schools, bilingual newspapers, radio and television stations, airlines, shipping companies, law firms, and scientific and medical operations.

While translators are employed nationwide, a large number of interpreters find work in New York and Washington, DC. Among the largest employers of interpreters and translators are the United Nations, the World Bank, the U.S. Department of State, the Bureau of the Census, the CIA, the FBI, the Library of Congress, the Red Cross, the YMCA, and the armed forces.

Finally, many interpreters and translators work independently in private practice. These self-employed professionals must be disciplined and driven, since they must handle all aspects of the business such as scheduling work and billing clients.

Starting Out

Most interpreters and translators begin as part-time freelancers until they gain experience and contacts in the field. Individuals can apply for jobs directly to the hiring firm, agency, or organization. Many of these employers advertise available positions in the classified section of the newspaper or on the Internet. In addition, contact your college placement office and language department to inquire about job leads.

While many opportunities exist, top interpreting and translating jobs are hard to obtain since the competition for these higher profile positions is fierce. You may be wise to develop supplemental skills that can be attractive to employers while honing your interpreting and translating techniques. The United Nations (UN), for example, employs administrative assistants who can take shorthand and transcribe notes in two or more languages. The UN also hires tour guides who speak more than one language. Such positions can be initial steps toward your future career goals.

Advancement

Competency in language determines the speed of advancement for interpreters and translators. Job opportunities and promotions are plentiful for those who have acquired great proficiency in languages. However, interpreters and translators need to constantly work and study to ensure that they keep abreast of the changing linguistic trends for a given language. The constant addition of new vocabulary for technological advances, inventions, and processes keep languages fluid. Those who do not keep up with changes will find that their communication skills become quickly outdated.

Interpreters and translators who work for government agencies advance by clearly defined grade promotions. Those who work for other organizations can aspire to become *chief interpreters* or *chief translators,* reviewers who check the work of others.

Although advancement in the field is generally slow, interpreters and translators will find many opportunities to advance as freelancers. Some can even establish their own bureaus or agencies.

Earnings

Earnings for interpreters and translators vary, depending on experience, skills, number of languages used, and employers. In government, trainee interpreters and translators generally begin at the GS-5 rating, earning from $21,947 to $28,535 a year in 2001. Those with a college degree can start at the higher GS-7 level, earning from $27,185 to $35,339. With an advanced degree, trainees begin at the GS-9 ($33,254 to $43,226), GS-10 ($36,621 to $47,610), or GS-11 level ($40,236 to $52,305).

Interpreters employed by the United Nations work under a salary structure called the Common System. These workers are usually paid higher than those working for the U.S. government, earning $28,341 to $60,000 a year in 2000.

Interpreters and translators who work on a freelance basis usually charge by the word, the page, the hour, or the project. Freelance interpreters for international conferences or meetings can earn between $300 and $500 a day from the U.S. government. By the hour, freelance translators usually earn between $15 and $35; however, rates vary depending on the language and the subject matter. Book translators work under contract with publishers. These contracts cover the fees that are to be paid for translating work as well as royalties, advances, penalties for late payments, and other provisions.

Interpreters and translators working in a specialized field have high earning potential. According to the National Association of Judiciary Interpreters and Translators, the federal courts paid $305 per day for court interpreters in 2000. Most work as freelancers, earning annual salaries from $30,000 to $80,000 a year.

Interpreters who work for the deaf also may work on a freelance basis, earning anywhere from $12 to $40 an hour, according to the Registry of Interpreters for the Deaf. Those employed with an agency, government organization, or school system can earn up to $30,000 to start; in urban areas, $40,000 to $50,000 a year.

Depending on the employer, interpreters and translators often enjoy such benefits as health and life insurance, pension plans, and paid vacation and sick days.

Work Environment

Interpreters and translators work under a wide variety of circumstances and conditions. As a result, most do not have typical nine-to-five schedules.

Conference interpreters probably have the most comfortable physical facilities in which to work. Their glass-enclosed booths are well lit and temperature controlled. Court or judiciary interpreters work in courtrooms or conference rooms, while interpreters for the deaf work at educational institutions as well as a wide variety of other locations.

Interpreters who work for escort or tour services are often required to travel for long periods of time. Their schedules are dictated by the group or person for whom they are interpreting. A freelance interpreter may work out of one city or be assigned anywhere in the world as needed.

Translators usually work in offices, although many spend considerable time in libraries and research centers. Freelance translators often work at home, using their own personal computers, modems, dictionaries, and other resource materials.

While both interpreting and translating require flexibility and versatility, interpreters in particular, especially those who work for international congresses or courts, may experience considerable stress and fatigue. Knowing that a great deal depends upon their absolute accuracy in interpretation can be a weighty responsibility.

Outlook

Employment opportunities for interpreters and translators are expected to grow about as fast as the average. However, competition for available positions will be fierce. With the explosion of such technologies as the Internet, lightning-fast modems, and videoconferencing, global communication has taken great strides. In short, the world has become smaller, so to speak, creating a demand for professionals to aid in the communication between people of different languages and cultural backgrounds.

In addition to new technological advances, demographic factors will fuel demand for translators and interpreters. Although some immigrants who come to the United States assimilate easily with respect to culture and language, many have difficulty learning English. As immigration into the country continues to increase, interpreters and translators will be needed to help immigrants function in an English-speaking society. According to Ann Macfarlane, president-elect of the American Translators Association, "community interpreting" for immigrants and refugees is a challenging area requiring qualified language professionals.

Another demographic factor influencing the interpreting and translating fields is the growth in overseas travel. Americans on average are spending an increasing amount of money on travel, especially to foreign countries. The resulting growth of the travel industry will create a need for interpreters to lead tours, both at home and abroad.

In addition to leisure travel, business travel is spurring the need for more translators and interpreters. With workers traveling abroad in growing numbers to attend meetings, conferences, and seminars with overseas clients, interpreters and translators will be needed to help bridge both the language and cultural gaps.

While no more than a few thousand interpreters and translators are employed in the largest markets (the federal government and international organizations), other job options exist. The medical field, for example, provides a variety of jobs for language professionals, translating such products as pharmaceutical inserts, research papers, and medical reports for insurance companies. Opportunities exist for qualified individuals in law, trade and business, health care, tourism, recreation, and the government.

For More Information

For more on the translating and interpreting professions, contact:

American Translators Association
225 Reinekers Lane, Suite 590
Alexandria, VA 22314
Tel: 703-683-6100
Email: ata@atanet.org
Web: http://www.atanet.org/

For information on linguistics programs, contact:

Georgetown University's Department of Linguistics
480 Intercultural Center
Washington, DC 20057-1051
Tel: 202-687-5956
Email: linguistics@gunet.georgetown.edu
Web: http://www.georgetown.edu/departments/linguistics/

For more information on court interpreting, contact:

National Association of Judiciary Interpreters and Translators
551 Fifth Avenue, Suite 3025
New York, NY 10176
Tel: 212-692-9581
Email: headquarters@najit.org
Web: http://www.najit.org

For information on working with the deaf, contact:

Registry of Interpreters for the Deaf, Inc.
333 Commerce Street
Alexandria, VA 22314
Tel: 703-838-0030
Web: http://www.rid.org

For information on foreign language careers with the federal government, including scholarship opportunities, contact:

Society of Federal Linguists
PO Box 7765
Washington, DC 20044
Web: http://www.federal-linguists.org

Museum Attendants and Teachers

English Sociology	School Subjects
Communication/ideas Helping/teaching	Personal Skills
Primarily indoors Primarily one location	Work Environment
High school diploma	Minimum Education Level
$10,000 to $25,000 to $36,000	Salary Range
None available	Certification or Licensing
Little change or more slowly than the average	Outlook

Overview

Museum attendants monitor exhibits, inform and guide visitors, and facilitate interactions between visitors and exhibits. They are the foremost representatives of the museum to the visiting public. The precise duties of a museum attendant vary with the needs of the museum and the specific job title. At some institutions, volunteers rather than employees may fulfill the duties of attendants. At others, attendants may function part-time in other areas of museum operations, such as in shipping and receiving, as sales clerks, or as library aides. In small museums, an attendant's duties may merge with those of the professional staff; in the smallest museums, the attendant may also be the director.

Museum teachers also provide information, share insight, and offer explanations of exhibits. Direct communication ranges from informal explanations at staff previews of a new exhibit, to addressing corporate donor groups, to aiding groups of schoolchildren. Museum teachers may write exhibit labels, prepare catalogs, or contribute to multimedia installations. Museum teachers also teach by demonstration, by conducting studio classes, or by leading field trips.

History

Museums in the United States not only display unusual or beautiful objects but also educate visitors in the historical, cultural, and scientific circumstances in which such objects came into existence. It is also of great importance to educate visitors about objects' modes of production, their relationship to similar objects, and the place of humans in an intercultural and biological universe.

Early museums in the United States were private collections staffed by their owner or the owner's family. In such cases, the owner often served as director, attendant, preparator, curator, publicist, and carpenter. An early, successful owner-attendant, Charles Willson Peale (1741-1827), is generally credited with starting the first natural history museum in postcolonial North America, the Philadelphia Museum, which opened in 1786. He exhibited specimens in naturalistic settings, against backdrops he had painted. His museum became an unofficial repository for specimens acquired on western trips of exploration, such as Meriwether Lewis (1774-1809) and William Clark's (1770-1838) expedition. Peale may also have begun the practice of printing catalogs of his holdings and reissuing them from time to time as the number of specimens increased or as more accurate identifications became available. Peale was not only the director of the museum but also its chief attendant and educator. He had irreproducible knowledge of the specimens, their origins, and their potential contributions to the state of science in the United States. He spread this knowledge freely through informal chats with visitors, publications, and correspondence with European collectors. The techniques Peale pioneered and his ideas about exhibition defined directions for U.S. museums for the next century.

As U.S. museums grew in size, scope, and operating budget, institutions such as the Museum of Fine Arts in Boston and the Field Museum of Natural History in Chicago were founded and housed in massive Greek-influenced structures during the late 19th century. However, the growth of these large museums did not adversely affect the development of small community- or family-owned museums. Attendants of such small museums may also serve as directors, or may be unpaid volunteers. As they go about their daily business, these attendants replicate many of the daily functions of the early directors of U.S. museums.

The Job

Like museum teachers, museum attendants often work through the education department or through a unit known as visitor services. In general, there are three levels of activity or authority, although all three levels are likely to exist formally only in the largest museums.

The role of museum teachers serving as *docents* or *interpreters,* is primarily based on interacting with visitors. In many museums, this position may be filled by museum attendants. Docents also give prepared talks or provide information in a loosely structured format, asking and answering questions informally. Good content knowledge is required, as well as sensitivity to visitor group composition and the ability to convey information to different types of audiences. Scholarly researchers, for example, have a different knowledge base and attention span than children.

Other museum teachers, such as *storytellers,* may be self-employed people who contract with a museum to provide special programs a few times a year. Many teachers are volunteers or part-time workers.

Education specialists are experts in a particular field, which may be education itself or an area in which the museum has large holdings, such as Asian textiles, North American fossils, or pre-Columbian pottery. Education specialists divide their time between planning programs and direct teaching. They may supervise other teachers, conduct field trips, or teach classes in local schools as part of joint programs of study between museums and schools.

Education directors, sometimes called *education officers,* administer their department and apply educational philosophies to the design of programs for different sectors of the public. They work closely with other museum staff, such as exhibit designers, librarians, and curators, and may have little direct contact with the public. In museums of all sizes, education directors may seek grant funding to support new exhibits. Some contribute papers to education journals or have responsibility for the museum's publications.

Museum attendants are sometimes called *museum aides.* A museum aide might also be a docent, or referred to as *guide* or *explainer.*

Receptionists greet visitors, collect admission fees, distribute maps, and answer general questions about exhibits and the layout of the museum. *Guards* primarily attend to the safety of the museum, its collections, its staff, and the overall flow of visitors. They observe public areas for hazards to visitors and evacuate the museum in case of emergencies. Some guards are cross-trained as *first-aid officers.* On a light visitor day, guards may act as on-the-spot *information officers.*

In another category of museum attendants are *gardeners* or *groundskeepers*. Ordinarily these functions are carried out by the museum's maintenance crew or by contract workers, but attendants may perform the task, especially if the museum is small and the grounds are considered an extension of the museum, such as the formal garden of a restored country house.

The functions of museum attendants vary with the size of the museum and its mission. Museums in the United States are as various as human interests. Among some of the lesser-known institutions are the Museum of Cartoon Art, the National Bottle Museum, roller skating and figure skating museums, museums of whaling, nuts, old fans, tattoo art, the Pony Express, locks, swimming, bullfighting, and butterflies. The position of attendant or educator in any one museum will not be exactly like that in any other museum, but some shared features of the work do exist. These features can be loosely sorted by type of museum.

In art museums attendants may deliver informative talks in a particular historical period as they accompany visitors through the exhibits, or they may be primarily concerned with the security of the collections. In natural history museums attendants describe the biological and evolutionary context of the specimens, how they were acquired by the museum, and the methods of preservation and mounting. In children's museums and space and technology museums, attendants are likely to be involved in hands-on, interactive activities throughout the working day. In folk museums or historical reconstructions, attendants may wear period clothing, demonstrate the use of antiquarian articles or older technologies such as spinning or milling, or they may prepare and serve food in a historically authentic manner.

Requirements

High School

Museum attendants and teachers must have working knowledge of their employing institution's collections. To achieve this wide range of knowledge, a broad academic background is necessary. Courses in art, biology, anthropology, archaeology, sociology, literature, and history are recommended. Math and computer courses are also beneficial because most museums are installing interactive computer displays in exhibit areas.

Postsecondary Training

Positions in museum teaching typically require content knowledge and teaching experience, which in turn are usually formalized through the acquisition of a bachelor's degree in an academic discipline or in education. Museum educators, who hold the position of director of education or education specialist, with accompanying budgetary, supervisory, and program development responsibilities, almost always need one or more advanced degrees.

Attendants typically undergo a period of in-service training immediately after being hired, during which they receive instruction in the content of the exhibits, the history of the museum, and in the specific duties they are expected to perform. Content instruction is repeated whenever a new exhibit opens or the attendant is shifted to a different area of the museum.

Other Requirements

Attendants and teachers are liaisons to the museum's visitors. Because museums strive to serve diverse audiences, museum attendants and teachers who know a foreign language, sign language, and/or CPR are at a great advantage. Being able to communicate with many types of individuals is a necessary requirement for these people-oriented positions.

Exploring

Because museum attendants interact with groups of visitors, activities such as leading organized clubs or groups, scouting groups, or travel societies will help you decide whether you would enjoy being a museum attendant. Comfort with public speaking, explaining, answering questions, and integrating new knowledge is an essential asset that can be developed through many avenues outside of the museum walls.

Many museums offer programs related to the museum's function, such as field trips, photography clubs, study groups, and behind-the-scenes tours. Volunteer positions for high school students are also available at many museums. Participation in such programs is a good way to become acquainted with the museum's scope and function and to observe firsthand the differences between museum teaching and traditional classroom teaching. College-age students may be eligible to apply for internships in a specific research or administrative area within a museum. The National Association for Interpretation sponsors workshops that address both practical and conceptual issues of interest to museum interpreters. Previous association with a museum in any capacity is an advantage when seeking employment in the museum field.

Employers

Museums, historical societies, libraries, zoos, botanical gardens, and state and federal agencies hire attendants and teachers. These institutions are located throughout the world, in both small and large cities, and are responsible for providing public access to their collections. Museums and similar institutions employ attendants and teachers to fulfill their educational goals while providing safe, pleasant environments for their visitors.

Starting Out

Although some colleges in the United States offer programs of instruction leading to a degree in museology (the study of museums), most museum workers at all levels enter museum work by virtue of possessing specific skills and knowledge needed by the museum. A teaching background or experience in leading activity groups are among the skills immediately transferable to a museum environment.

In general, the museum attendant position is not a professional position, and a high school degree may be sufficient for employment. Some institutions may give hiring preference to applicants with a bachelor's degree. Applicants with advanced degrees and relevant work experience, such as teaching, field work, or public relations, are usually better positioned to take advantage of employment opportunities in the museum field.

Many museums have a substantial volunteer staff, and this method of entering museum work should not be overlooked. Volunteering allows flexible hours and close observation of the different activities conducted in administrative, research, and exhibit areas.

Advancement

Museum work is characterized by unusual freedom within a job area and short, sometimes nonexistent, promotional ladders. For example, only one or two management levels may separate museum attendants from the director of the museum, yet the positions at the intervening levels may carry specific requirements, such as a bachelor's degree and several years of experience in managing budgets and staff. It is unlikely that an attendant lacking these qualifications would be able to acquire them solely through continuing work at the museum. There are no hard-and-fast rules, however. To offset the relative lack of vertical movement, there is more than usual opportunity for lateral movement, that is, for assuming a new position elsewhere in the museum at the same employment rank, and for exploring a position in depth. Attendants' duties may change with the seasons, as new exhibits are opened, and as attendants gain experience and discover creative possibilities in their jobs. Because of the stimulating and changing environment, museum workers tend to have high job satisfaction and may remain in their jobs for long periods of time; when they do move, they often remain within the museum field. Attendants who are successful at smaller museums may move to larger institutions with correspondingly broader responsibilities.

Attendants may continue their own education and acquire job skills relevant to an area of work they have identified as a career interest. These areas might include work as an education specialist; in museum operations, such as maintenance or exhibit preparation; in administration; or in public programs.

Museum teachers with experience and appropriate academic or teaching credentials may become *content specialists* in one area of the museum's collection or may become education directors, assuming responsibility for the departmental budget, educational policies and community outreach programs, and training and supervision of numerous staff and volunteer workers. Advancement may depend on acquisition of an advanced degree in education or in an academic field. Because professional supervisory positions are few in comparison to the large corps of teachers, museum teachers desiring advancement may need to look beyond their home institution, perhaps accepting a smaller salary at a smaller museum in return for a supervisory title.

Teachers who leave museum work are well positioned to seek employment elsewhere in the nonprofit sector, especially with grant-funding agencies involved in community-based programs. In the for-profit sector, excellent communication skills and the ability to express an institution's philosophy both in writing and in interviews are skills valued by the public relations departments of corporations.

Earnings

The range of compensation for museum positions is extremely broad, reflecting not only the museum's size, mission, operating budget, and staffing requirements, but the metropolitan area in which it is located. A 1997 study conducted by the Association of Art Museum Directors reported that the average salary of an educational assistant is roughly $22,000. The average salary of an assistant educator ranges from $25,000 to $32,000, while the average salary of an associate educator is roughly $36,000. Depending on full- or part-time employment status, museum attendants' salaries vary greatly, but typically begin at the rate of $5.15 to $6 per hour in institutions with operational budgets below $1,000,000.

Fringe benefits, including paid vacations and sick leave, medical and dental insurance, and retirement plans, vary between museum attendants and teachers. Benefit policies depend on employment status as well as on the operational budget and size of the employing institution.

Work Environment

Museum attendants spend long hours standing or walking about the museum, answering questions, directing visitors, and monitoring exhibits. Once trained, attendants frequently work without daily supervision, but must constantly be attentive to the public and courteous even when fatigued. Attendants are needed during all hours that a museum is open to the public and occasionally when museum space has been rented for a private function. Flexibility in working hours may be a requirement of employment. Company-paid medical and health insurance may not be available to part-time workers and may not be available even to full-time staff in small museums. Federal museums are more likely than nonfederal museums to offer health and retirement benefits.

Most museum attendants work within the museum, but some may assist on field trips or conduct programs in local schools. Some museum attendants live at the site.

Most museum teachers have a base of operation in the museum but may not have a private office, for the bulk of their work is carried out in exhibit areas, in resource centers or study rooms within the museum, in classrooms outside of the museum, or in the field. Permanent staff work a normal workweek, with occasional weekend or evening assignments.

Museum teaching varies from day to day and offers innovative teachers a chance to devise different programs. However, museum teaching is different from conventional classroom teaching where educators have the benefit of more time to convey ideas and facts.

Outlook

The public education services provided by museum attendants and educators are a core part of a museum's efforts to justify spending. That does not necessarily mean museum employment is high. Rather, greater professionalism will be expected at all levels of museum work, and efforts to recruit and train volunteers for specific tasks will likely increase.

Two conflicting factors are expected to shape the employment picture for museum attendants in the upcoming decade. The first is an increasing awareness of the global environment and an emphasis on intercultural understanding. The second factor is the slowing of the nation's economy and institutions' caution in initiating new job positions. As a result, the employment of museum attendants and teachers is expected to change little or grow more slowly that the average for all occupations through 2008.

For More Information

For information on careers, education, training, and internships, contact the following organizations:

American Association of Museums
1575 Eye Street, NW, Suite 400
Washington, DC 20005
Tel: 202-289-1818
Web: http://www.aam-us.org

Association of Art Museum Directors
41 East 65th Street
New York, NY 10021
Tel: 212-249-4423
Web: http://www.aamd.org

For information on student memberships, contact:

National Art Education Association
1916 Association Drive
Reston, VA 20191
Tel: 703-860-8000
Email: naea@dgs.dgsys.com
Web: http://www.naea-reston.org

For information regarding workshops for museum interpreters and docents, contact:

National Association for Interpretation
PO Box 2246
Fort Collins, CO 80522
Tel: 888-900-8283
Email: membership@interpnet.com
Web: http://www.interpnet.com

Naturalists

Biology Earth science	School Subjects
Communication/ideas Technical/scientific	Personal Skills
Primarily outdoors One location with some travel	Work Environment
Bachelor's degree	Minimum Education Level
$15,000 to $25,000 to $70,000	Salary Range
None available	Certification or Licensing
About as fast as the average	Outlook

Overview

The primary role of *naturalists* is to educate the public about the environment and maintain the natural environment on land specifically dedicated to wilderness populations. Their primary responsibilities are preserving, restoring, maintaining, and protecting a natural habitat. Among the related responsibilities in these jobs are teaching, public speaking, writing, giving scientific and ecological demonstrations, and handling public relations and administrative tasks. Naturalists may work in a variety of environments, including private nature centers; local, state, and national parks and forests; wildlife museums; and independent nonprofit conservation and restoration associations. Some of the many job titles a naturalist might hold are fish and game warden, fish and wildlife officer, land steward, wildlife biologist, and environmental interpreter. Natural resource managers, wildlife conservationists, and ecologists sometimes perform the work of naturalists.

History

Prior to the 17th century, there was little support for environmental preservation. Instead, wilderness was commonly seen as a vast resource to be controlled. This view began to change during the early years of the Industrial Revolution, when new energy resources were utilized, establishing an increasing need for petroleum, coal, natural gas, wood, and water for hydropowered energy. In England and France, for example, the rapid depletion of natural forests caused by the increased use of timber for powering the new industries led to demands for forest conservation.

The United States, especially during the 19th century, saw many of its great forests razed, huge tracts of land leveled for open-pit mining and quarrying, and increased disease with the rise of air pollution from the smokestacks of factories, home chimneys, and engine exhaust. Much of the land damage occurred at the same time as a dramatic depletion of wildlife, including elk, antelope, deer, bison, and other animals of the Great Plains. Some types of bear, cougar, and wolf became extinct, as did several kinds of birds, such as the passenger pigeon. In the latter half of the 19th century, the U.S. government set up a commission to develop scientific management of fisheries, established the first national park (Yellowstone National Park in Wyoming), and set aside the first forest reserves. The modern conservation movement grew out of these early steps.

States also established parks and forests for wilderness conservation. Parks and forests became places where people, especially urban dwellers, could acquaint themselves with the natural settings of their ancestors. Naturalists, employed by the government, institutions of higher education, and various private concerns, were involved not only in preserving and exploring the natural reserves but also in educating the public about the remaining wilderness.

Controversy over the proper role of U.S. parks and forests began soon after their creation (and continues to this day), as the value of these natural areas for logging, recreation, and other human activities conflicted with the ecological need for preservation. President Theodore Roosevelt, a strong supporter of the conservation movement, believed nevertheless in limited industrial projects, such as dams, within the wilderness areas. Despite the controversy, the system of national parks and forests expanded throughout the 20th century. Today, the Agriculture and Interior Departments, and to a lesser extent the Department of Defense, have conservation responsibilities for soil, forests, grasslands, water, wildlife, and federally owned land.

In the 1960s and early 1970s, the hazards posed by pollution to both humans and the environment highlighted the importance of nature preservation and public education. Federal agencies were established, such as the

Environmental Protection Agency, the Council on Environmental Quality, and the National Oceanic and Atmospheric Administration. Crucial legislation was passed, including the Wilderness Act (1964) and the Endangered Species Act (1969). Naturalists have been closely involved with these conservation efforts and others, shouldering the responsibility to communicate to the public the importance of maintaining diverse ecosystems and to help restore or balance ecosystems under threat.

The Job

Because of the impact of human populations on the environment, virtually no area in the United States is truly wild. Land and the animal populations require human intervention to help battle against the human encroachment that is damaging or hindering wildlife. Naturalists work to help wildlife maintain or improve their hold in the world.

The work can be directly involved in maintaining individual populations of animals or plants, overseeing whole ecosystems, or promoting the work of those who are directly involved in the maintenance of the ecosystem. Fish and wildlife officers (or fish and game wardens) work to preserve and restore the animal populations, including migratory birds that may only be part of the environment temporarily. Wildlife managers and range conservationists oversee the combination of plants and animals in their territories.

Fish and wildlife officers study, assist, and help regulate the populations of fish, hunted animals, and protected animals throughout the United States. They may work directly in the parks and reserves or they may oversee a region within a particular state, even if there are no park lands there. *Fish and game wardens* control the hunting and fishing of wild populations to make sure that the populations are not overharvested during a season. They monitor the populations of each species off season as well as make sure the species is thriving but is not overpopulating and running the risk of starvation or territory damage. Most people hear about the fish and game wardens when a population of animals has overgrown its territory and needs either to be culled (selectively hunted) or moved. Usually this occurs with the deer population, but it can also apply to predator animals such as the coyote or fox, or scavenger animals such as the raccoon. Because the practice of culling animal populations arouses controversy, the local press usually gives wide coverage to such situations.

The other common time to hear about wildlife wardens is when poaching is uncovered locally. Poaching can be hunting or fishing an animal out of season or hunting or fishing a protected animal. Although we think of poachers in the African plains hunting lions and elephants, poaching is common in the United States for animals such as mountain lions, brown bears, eagles, and wolves. Game wardens target and arrest poachers; punishment can include prison sentences and steep fines.

Wildlife managers, range managers, and *conservationists* work to maintain the plant and animal life in a given area. Wildlife managers can work in small local parks or enormous national parks. Range managers work on ranges that have a combination of domestic livestock and wild population. The U.S. government has leased and permitted farmers to graze and raise livestock on federally held ranges, although this program is under increasing attack by conservationists. Range managers must ensure that both the domestic and wild populations are living side by side successfully. They make sure that the population of predatory wild animals does not increase enough to deplete the livestock and that the livestock does not overgraze the land and eliminate essential food for the wild animals. Range managers and conservationists must test soil and water for nutrients and pollution, count plant and animal populations in every season, and keep in contact with farmers using the land for reports of attacks on livestock or the presence of disease.

Wildlife managers also balance the needs of the humans using or traveling through the land they supervise and the animals that live in or travel through that same land. They keep track of the populations of animals and plants and provide food and water when it is lacking naturally. This may involve airdrops of hay and grain during winter months to deer, moose, or elk populations in remote reaches of a national forest, or digging and filling a water reservoir for animals during a drought.

Naturalists in all these positions often have administrative duties such as supervising staff members and volunteers, raising funds (particularly for independent nonprofit organizations), writing grant applications, taking and keeping records and statistics, and maintaining public relations. They may write articles for local or national publications to inform and educate the public about their location or a specific project. They may be interviewed by journalists for reports concerning their site or their work.

Nature walks are often given to groups as a way of educating people about the land and the work that goes into revitalizing and maintaining it. Tourists, schoolchildren, amateur conservationists and naturalists, social clubs, and retirees commonly attend these walks. On a nature walk, the naturalist may point out specific plants and animals, identify rocks, and discuss soil composition or the natural history of the area (including special environmental strengths and problems). The naturalist may even discuss the indigenous people of the area, especially in terms of how they adapted to the unique aspects of their particular environment. Because such a variety of topics may be brought up, the naturalist must be an environmental generalist, familiar with such subjects as biology, botany, geology, geography, meteorology, anthropology, and history.

Naturalists use demonstrations, exhibits, and classes to educate the public about the environment. For example, to help children understand oil spills, the naturalist may set up a simple demonstration showing that oil and water do not mix. Instruction may also be given on outdoor activities, such as hiking and camping.

For some naturalists, preparing educational materials is a large part of their job. Brochures, fact sheets, pamphlets, and newsletters may be written for people visiting the park or nature center. Materials might also be sent to area residents in an effort to gain public support.

One aspect of protecting any natural area involves communicating facts and debunking myths about how to respect the area and the flora and fauna that inhabit it. Another aspect involves tending managed areas to promote a diversity of plants and animals. This may mean introducing trails and footpaths that provide easy yet noninvasive access for the public; it may mean cordoning off an area to prevent foot traffic from ruining a patch of rare moss; or it may mean instigating a letter-writing campaign to drum up support for legislation to protect a specific area, plant, or animal. It may be easy to get support for protecting the snowshoe rabbit; it is harder to make the public understand the need to preserve and maintain a batcave.

Some naturalists, such as directors of nature centers or conservation organizations, have massive administrative responsibilities. They might recruit volunteers and supervise staff, organize long- and short-term program goals, and handle record-keeping and the budget. To raise money, naturalists may need to speak publicly on a regular basis, write grant proposals, and organize and attend scheduled fund-raising activities and community meetings. Naturalists also try to increase public awareness and support by writing press releases and organizing public workshops, conferences, seminars, meetings, and hearings. In general, naturalists must be available as resources for educating and advising the community.

Requirements

High School

High school students interested in the field should consider taking a number of basic science courses, including biology and chemistry. Botany courses and clubs are helpful, since they provide direct experience monitoring plant growth and health. Animal care experience, usually obtained through volunteer work, also is helpful.

Postsecondary Training

An undergraduate degree in environmental, physical, or natural sciences is generally the minimum educational requirement for becoming a naturalist. Common college majors are biology, forestry, wildlife management, natural resource and park management, natural resources, botany, zoology, chemistry, natural history, and environmental science. Course work in economics, history, anthropology, English, international studies, and communication arts are also helpful.

Graduate education is increasingly required for employment as a naturalist, particularly for upper level positions. A master's degree in natural science or natural resources is the minimum requirement for supervisory or administrative roles in many of the nonprofit agencies, and several positions require either a doctorate or several years of experience in the field. For positions in agencies with international sites, work abroad is necessary and can be obtained through volunteer positions such as those with the Peace Corps or in paid positions assisting in site administration and management.

Other Requirements

Those considering careers in this field should like working outdoors, as most naturalists spend the majority of their time outside in all kinds of weather. However, along with the desire to work in and with the natural world, the naturalist needs to be capable of communicating with the human world as well. Excellent writing skills are helpful in preparing educational materials and grant proposals.

For people working in the field, seemingly unrelated skills such as engine repair and basic carpentry can be essential to managing a post. Because of the remote locations of many of the work sites, self-sufficiency in operating and maintaining the equipment allows the staff to lose fewer days because of equipment breakdown.

Exploring

One of the best ways to learn about the job of a naturalist is to volunteer at one of the many national and state parks or nature centers. These institutions often recruit volunteers for outdoor work. College students, for example, are sometimes hired to work as summer or part-time nature guides. Outdoor recreation and training organizations, such as Outward Bound and the National Outdoor Leadership School, are especially good resources. Most volunteer positions, though, require a high school diploma and some college credit.

Students should also consider college internship programs. In addition, conservation programs and organizations throughout the country and the world offer opportunities for volunteer work in a wide variety of areas, including working with the public, giving lectures and guided tours, and working with others to build or maintain an ecosystem.

You can also explore the naturalist careers online; two Web sites to check out are environmental-jobs.com and ecojobs.com.

Starting Out

For park employees, the usual method of entry is through part-time or seasonal employment for the first several jobs, then a full-time position. Because it is difficult to get experience before completing a college degree, and because seasonal employment is common, students interested in this career path should prepare to seek supplemental income for their first few years in the field.

International experience is helpful with agencies that work beyond the U.S. borders. This can be through the Peace Corps or other volunteer organizations that work with local populations on land and habitat management or restoration. Other volunteer experience is available through local restoration programs on sites in your area. Organizations such as the Nature Conservancy, Open Lands, and many others buy land to restore, and these organizations rely extensively on volunteer labor for stewarding and working the land. Rescue and release centers work with injured and abandoned wildlife to rehabilitate them. Opportunities at these centers can include banding wild animals for tracking, working with injured or adolescent animals for release training, and adapting unreleasable animals to educational programs and presentations.

Advancement

In some settings, such as small nature centers, there may be little room for advancement. In larger organizations, experience and additional education can lead to increased responsibility and pay. Among the higher-level positions is that of director, handling supervisory, administrative, and public relations tasks.

Advancement into upper-level management and supervisory positions usually requires a graduate degree, although people with a graduate degree and no work experience will still have to start in nearly entry-level positions. So you can either work a few years and then return to school to get an advanced degree or complete your education and start in the same position as you would have without the degree. The advanced degree will allow you eventually to move further up in the organizational structure.

Earnings

Starting salaries for full-time naturalists range from about $15,000 to $22,000 per year. Some part-time workers, however, make as little as minimum wage. For some positions, housing and vehicles may be provided. Earnings vary for those with added responsibilities or advanced degrees. Field officers and supervisors make between $25,000 and $45,000 a year, and upper management employees can make between $30,000 and $70,000, depending on the organization.

Work Environment

Naturalists spend a majority of their working hours outdoors. Depending on the location, the naturalist must work in a wide variety of weather conditions: from frigid cold to sweltering heat to torrential rain. Remote sites are common, and long periods of working either in isolation or in small teams is not uncommon for field research and management. Heavy lifting, hauling, working with machinery and hand tools, digging, planting, harvesting, and tracking may fall to the naturalist working in the field. One wildlife manager in Montana spent every daylight hour for several days in a row literally running up and down snow-covered mountains, attempting to tranquilize and collar a mountain lion. Clearly, this can be a physically demanding job.

Indoor work includes scheduling, planning, and classroom teaching. Data gathering and maintaining logs and records are required for many jobs. Naturalists may need to attend and speak at local community meetings. They may have to read detailed legislative bills to analyze the impact of legislation before it becomes law.

Those in supervisory positions, such as directors, are often so busy with administrative and organizational tasks that they may spend little of their workday outdoors. Work that includes guided tours and walks through nature areas is frequently seasonal and usually dependent on daily visitors.

Full-time naturalists usually work about 35 to 40 hours per week. Overtime is usually required, and for those naturalists working in areas visited by campers, camping season is extremely busy and can require much overtime. Wildlife and range managers may be on call during storms and severe weather. Seasonal work, such as burn season for land managers and stewards, may require overtime and frequent weekend work.

Naturalists have special occupational hazards, such as working with helicopters, small airplanes, all-terrain vehicles, and other modes of transport through rugged landscapes and into remote regions. Adverse weather conditions and working in rough terrain make illness and injury more likely. Naturalists must be able to get along with the variety of people using the area and may encounter armed individuals who are poaching or otherwise violating the law.

Naturalists also have a number of unique benefits. Most prominent is the chance to live and work in some of the most beautiful places in the world. For many individuals, the lower salaries are offset by the recreational and lifestyle opportunities afforded by living and working in such scenic areas. In general, occupational stress is low, and most naturalists appreciate the opportunity to continually learn about and work to improve the environment.

Outlook

The outlook for naturalists is expected to be fair in the first decade of the 21st century. While a growing public concern about environmental issues may cause an increased demand for naturalists, this trend could be offset by government cutbacks in nature programs. Reduced government spending on education may indirectly affect the demand for naturalists, as school districts would have less money to spend on outdoor education and recreation. Despite the limited number of available positions, the number of well-qualified applicants is expected to remain high.

For More Information

For information on environmental expeditions, contact:

Earthwatch Expeditions, Inc.
PO Box 75
Maynard, MA 01754-0075
Tel: 978-461-0081
Web: http://www.earthwatch.org/

*For information about internships, career conferences, and publications, such as
the* **Environmental Career Resources Guide,** *contact:*

Environmental Careers Organization
179 South Street
Boston, MA 02111
Tel: 617-426-4375
Web: http://www.eco.org/

*This group offers internships and fellowships for college and graduate students
with an interest in environmental issues. For information, contact:*

Friends of the Earth
1025 Vermont Avenue, NW
Washington, DC 20005
Tel: 877-843-8687
Email: foe@foe.org
Web: http://www.foe.org

*For information on environmental issues, services, events, news, and job listings,
check out the following Web sites:*

Earth Force
1908 Mount Vernon, Second Floor
Alexandria, VA 22301
Tel: 703-299-9400
Email: earthforce@earthforce.org
Web: http://www.earthforce.org/

Institute for Global Communications
18 DeBoom Street
San Francisco, CA 94107
Tel: 415-442-0220
Web: http://www.econet.org

National Wildlife Federation
11100 Wildlife Center Drive
Reston, VA 20190-5362
Tel: 800-822-9919
Web: http://www.nwf.org

For information on animals, education, world news, and other fun facts, check out the following Web site created by the Wildlife Conservation Association:

Kids Go Wild
Web: http://wcs.org/sites/kidsgowild

Nursing Instructors

Biology
Chemistry — School Subjects

Helping/teaching
Technical/scientific — Personal Interests

Primarily indoors
Primarily multiple locations — Work Environment

Bachelor's degree — Minimum Education Level

$16,000 to $50,000 to $140,000 — Salary Range

Required by all states — Certification or Licensing

Faster than the average — Outlook

Overview

Nursing instructors teach patient care to nursing students in classroom and clinical settings. They demonstrate care methods and monitor hands-on learning by their students. They instruct students in the principles and applications of biological and psychological subjects related to nursing. Some nursing instructors specialize in teaching specific areas of nursing such as surgical or oncological nursing.

Nursing instructors may be full professors, assistant professors, instructors, or lecturers depending on their education and the facilities' nursing programs.

History

In 1873, the first school of nursing in the United States was founded in Boston. In 1938, New York state passed the first law requiring that practical nurses be licensed. Even though the first school for the training of practical nurses had been started almost 75 years before, and the establishment of other schools followed, the training programs lacked uniformity.

Shortly after licensure requirements surfaced, a movement towards organized training programs began that would help to ensure quality standards in the field. The role and training of the nurse have undergone radical changes since the first nursing schools were opened.

Education standards for nurses have been improving constantly since that time. Nurses are now required by all states to be appropriately educated and licensed to practice. Extended programs of training are offered throughout the country. The field of nursing serves an important role as a part of the health care system.

According to the American Association of Colleges of Nursing (AACN), the field of nursing is the nation's largest health care profession, with more than 2.5 million *registered nurses* (RNs) nationwide. Of all licensed RNs, 2.1 million, or 83 percent, are employed in nursing.

Nursing students account for more than half of all health professions students in the United States. However, the changes in the health care system are affecting nursing education. Despite a growing demand for nursing professionals, there has been a constant decline in program enrollments since 1995, according to reports by the AACN. Several factors for these low enrollment numbers are involved. Bachelor's degree nursing programs have had difficulty in attracting qualified faculty. Budgetary limitations, competition with clinical service agencies, and lack of qualified nursing instructors have reduced the number of quality instructors. A lack of classroom space and clinical training sites, also highly sought after due to the emphasis on community-based services, also limit the number of nursing educators.

The Job

Nursing instructors teach in colleges and universities, or nursing schools. They teach in classrooms and in clinical settings. Their duties depend on the facility, the nursing program, and the instructor's education level. Some nursing instructors specialize in specific subjects such as chemistry or anatomy, or in a type of nursing activity such as pediatric nursing.

Many health care facilities partner with area nursing programs so the students can actually practice what they are learning under the supervision of nursing staff and instructors. For example, the students may spend time in a hospital environment learning pediatrics and surgical care, and additional time in a nursing home setting learning the health care needs of the elderly and handicapped. Classroom instruction and clinical training depend on the nursing program and the degree conferred.

Mary Bell, R.N., who has 12 years of nursing experience, taught classes part-time as an associate professor in Indiana. Classroom teaching and clinical practice were her responsibilities.

Bell says, "As part of the clinical instruction, students conferred with me regarding the patients. They assessed the patients and learned how to chart information and statistics. Sometimes their patient observations were very keen."

"I loved the clinical part of teaching," she says. "The students often brought a new perspective to nursing. They were always eager to learn and to share what they learned.

"Nursing technology and care is always changing and the instructor shouldn't mind being challenged," states Bell. She goes on to say that the instructor must be able to create dialogue so there is an exchange of information and ideas. "It is a process between student and teacher," she observes.

Nursing instructors must spend a lot of preparation time outside the classroom and clinical setting, according to Bell. For example, the instructor must work with head nurses or charge nurses to determine the students' patient assignments. They must review patients' charts and be well informed about their current conditions prior to the student nurses appearing for their clinical instruction. Plus, there are the usual teaching responsibilities such as course planning, paper grading, and test preparation. Involvement often extends beyond the classroom.

"Professors at universities and colleges are expected to be involved with the community," says Bell. They may be required to speak to community groups or consult with businesses, and are encouraged to be active in professional associations and on academic committees.

"In addition, many larger institutions expect professors to do research and be published in nursing or medical journals," Bell notes.

Teaching load and research requirements vary by institution and program. Full professors usually spend more of their time conducting research and publishing than assistant professors, instructors, and lecturers.

Often nursing instructors actively work in the nursing field along with teaching. "They will do this to maintain current hands-on experience and to advance their careers," Bell acknowledges. "It is a huge commitment."

"But," she adds, "it's great being able to see the light bulb turn on in the students' heads."

Requirements

High School

If you are interested in becoming a nursing instructor, take classes in health and the sciences to prepare you for a medical career. Since nursing instructors begin as nurses themselves, you need to take classes that will prepare you for nursing programs. Biology, chemistry, mathematics, and English courses will help you build the strong foundation necessary for nursing school.

Postsecondary Training

Most nursing instructors first work as registered nurses and, therefore, obtain either a two- or three-year associate's degree, or a four-year bachelor's degree in nursing. Nursing instructors should also have considerable clinical nursing experience before considering teaching.

Most universities and colleges require that their full-time professors have doctoral degrees, but many hire master's degree holders for part-time and temporary teaching positions. Two-year colleges may hire full-time teachers who have master's degrees. Smaller institutions or nursing schools may hire part-time nursing instructors who have a bachelor's degree.

Certification or Licensing

In order to practice as a registered nurse, you first must become licensed in the state in which you plan to work. Licensed RNs must graduate from an accredited school of nursing and pass a national examination. In order to renew their license, RNs must show proof of continued education and pass renewal exams. Most states honor licenses granted in other states, so long as scores are acceptable.

Other Requirements

Nursing instructors must enjoy teaching and nursing. They should have excellent organizational and leadership skills, and be able to communicate well with professional staff and students of all ages. They should be able to demonstrate skilled nursing techniques. They must have good supervision skills since they are responsible for all the care their students administer to patients. In addition, they should be able to teach their students the humane side of nursing that is so important in patient and nurse relationships. New medical technologies, patient treatments, and medications are constantly being developed, so nursing instructors must stay abreast of new information in the medical field. They need to be up-to-date on the use of new medical equipment that is used for patient care.

Exploring

While in high school, you can explore your interest in the nursing field in a number of ways. Consult your high school guidance counselor, school nurse, and local community nurses for information. A visit to a hospital or nursing clinic can give you a chance to observe the roles and duties of nurses in the facility and may give you the opportunity to talk one-on-one with staff members. Check to see if you can volunteer to work in a hospital, nursing home, or clinic after school, on weekends, or during summer vacation to further explore your interest.

To get a better sense of the teaching work involved in being a nursing instructor, explore your interest and talents as a teacher. Spend some time with one of your teachers after school and ask to look at lecture notes and record-keeping procedures. Ask your teacher about the amount of work that goes into preparing a class or directing an extracurricular activity. To get some firsthand teaching experience, volunteer for a peer tutoring program.

Employers

Nursing instructors work in hospitals, clinics, colleges, and universities that offer nursing education programs. Instructors' jobs can vary greatly, depending on the employer. Many nursing instructors associated with hospitals or medical clinics work in the nursing field in addition to teaching. Those employed by large universities and colleges are more focused on academia, conducting medical research and writing medical reports of their findings.

Starting Out

Because nursing instructors first obtain practical experience in the field, set your sights on becoming a registered nurse. After graduating from an approved nursing program and passing licensure examinations, apply for employment directly to hospitals, nursing homes, companies, and government agencies that hire nurses. Jobs can also be obtained through school placement offices, employment agencies specializing in placement of nursing personnel, or through your state's employment office. Other sources of jobs include nurses' associations, professional journals, and newspaper want ads.

Advancement

In hospitals and clinics, nursing instructors generally advance by moving up in staff ranks. Positions with higher levels of authority, and hence, higher pay, include clinical nurse specialists, advanced practice nurses, nurse supervisors, or medical administrators.

Those who work in nursing schools, colleges, or universities may advance from a part-time to a full-time faculty position. As they advance their careers, many full-time instructors spend less time in the classroom and more time conducting research, public speaking, and writing.

Earnings

Educational background, experience, responsibilities, geographic location, and the hiring institution determine the earnings as a nursing instructor.

According to a survey conducted in 1998 by the American Association of Colleges of Nursing, the salaries for nursing instructors with doctoral degrees ranged from $26,000 in a public institution to $138,175 for a professor in a private secular school. Salaries for instructors who did not have doctorates ranged from $16,102 to $89,771. The survey also noted that salaries vary by type of institution and geographic location.

Employers usually provide health and life insurance and other benefits to their full-time employees.

Work Environment

Nursing instructors work in colleges, universities, or nursing schools. Their clinical instruction can take place in doctors' offices, medical clinics, hospitals, institutions, and nursing homes. Most health care environments are clean and well lighted. Inner-city facilities may be in rough locations and safety may be an issue.

All health-related careers have some health and disease risks; however, adherence to health and safety guidelines greatly minimizes the chance of contracting infectious diseases such as hepatitis and AIDS. Safety measures are also needed to limit exposure to toxic chemicals, radiation, and other hazards.

Outlook

Nursing specialties will be in great demand in the future, thus creating a demand for nursing instructors. The U.S. Bureau of Labor Statistics lists nursing as one of 10 occupations with the largest growth rate. From 1998 to 2008, jobs for registered nurses are expected to increase by 21.6 percent. The bureau also reports that health services is one of the largest industries in the country, and that 12 out of 30 occupations projected to grow the fastest are concentrated in health services. These facts support the need for nurse instructors today and in the future.

For More Information

For more information, contact the following organizations:

American Association of Colleges of Nursing
One Dupont Circle, NW, Suite 530
Washington, DC 20036
Tel: 202-463-6930
Web: http://www.aacn.nche.edu

American Nurses Association
600 Maryland Avenue, SW, Suite 100W
Washington, DC 20024
Tel: 800-274-4262
Web: http://www.ana.org

Park Rangers

School Subjects	Earth science Geography
Personal Skills	Helping/teaching Leadership/management
Work Environment	Indoors and outdoors Primarily multiple locations
Minimum Education Level	Bachelor's degree
Salary Range	$21,947 to $33,254 to $43,000+
Certification or Licensing	None available
Outlook	Little change or more slowly than the average

Overview

Park rangers enforce laws and regulations in national, state, and county parks. They help care for and maintain parks as well as inform, guide, and ensure the safety of park visitors.

History

The National Park System in the United States was begun by Congress in 1872 when Yellowstone National Park was created. The National Park Service (NPS), a bureau of the U.S. Department of the Interior, was created in 1916 to preserve, protect, and manage the national, cultural, historical, and recreational areas of the National Park System. At that time, the park system contained less than 1 million acres. Today, the country's national parks cover more than 80.7 million acres of mountains, plains, deserts, swamps, historic sites, lakeshores, forests, rivers, battlefields, memorials, archaeological properties, and recreation areas.

All NPS areas are given one of the following designations: National Park, National Historical Park, National Battlefield, National Battlefield Park, National Battlefield Site, National Military Site, National Memorial, National Historic Site, National Monument, National Preserve, National Seashore, National Parkway, National Lakeshore, National Reserve, National River, National Wild and Scenic River, National Recreation Area, or just Park. (The White House in Washington, DC, for example, which is administered by the NPS, is officially a Park.)

To protect the fragile, irreplaceable resources located in these areas, and to protect the millions of visitors who climb, ski, hike, boat, fish, and otherwise explore them, the National Park Service employs park rangers. State and county parks employ rangers to perform similar tasks.

The Job

Park rangers have a wide variety of duties that range from conservation efforts to bookkeeping. Their first responsibility is, however, safety. Rangers who work in parks with treacherous terrain, dangerous wildlife, or severe weather must make sure hikers, campers, and backpackers follow outdoor safety codes. They often require visitors to register at park offices so that rangers will know when someone does not return from a hike or climb and may be hurt. Rangers often participate in search-and-rescue missions for visitors who are lost or injured in parks. In mountainous or forested regions, they may use helicopters or horses for searches.

Rangers also protect parks from inappropriate use and other threats from humans. They register vehicles and collect parking and registration fees, which are used to help maintain roads and facilities. They enforce the laws, regulations, and policies of the parks, patrolling to prevent vandalism, theft, and harm to wildlife. Rangers may arrest and evict people who violate these laws. Some of their efforts to conserve and protect park resources include keeping jeeps and other motorized vehicles off sand dunes and other fragile lands. They make sure visitors do not litter, pollute water, chop down trees for firewood, or start unsafe campfires that could lead to catastrophic forest fires. When forest fires do start, rangers often help with the dangerous, arduous task of putting them out.

Park rangers carry out various tasks associated with the management of the natural resources within our National Park System. An important aspect of this responsibility is the care and management of both native and exotic animal species found within the boundaries of the parks. Duties may include conducting basic research, as well as disseminating information about the reintroduction of native animal populations and the protection of the natural habitat that supports the animals.

Rangers also help with conservation, research, and ecology efforts that are not connected to visitors' use of the park. They may study wildlife behavior patterns, for example, by tagging and following certain animals. In this way, they can chart the animals' migration patterns, assess the animals' impact on the park's ecosystem, and determine whether the park should take measures to control or encourage certain wildlife populations.

Some rangers study plant life and may work with conservationists to reintroduce native or endangered species. They measure the quality of water and air in the park to monitor and mitigate the effects of pollution and other threats from sources outside park boundaries.

In addition, park rangers help visitors enjoy and experience parks. In historical and other cultural parks, such as the Alamo in San Antonio, Independence Hall in Philadelphia, and the Lincoln Home in Springfield, Illinois, rangers give lectures and provide guided tours explaining the history and significance of the site. In natural parks, they may lecture on conservation topics, provide information about plants and animals in the park, and take visitors on interpretive walks, pointing out the area's flora, fauna, and geological characteristics. At a Civil War battlefield park, such as Gettysburg National Military Park in Pennsylvania or Vicksburg National Military Park in Mississippi, they explain to visitors what happened at that site during the Civil War and its implications for our country.

Park rangers are also indispensable to the management and administration of parks. They issue permits to visitors and vehicles and help plan the recreational activities in parks. They help in the planning and managing of park budgets. They keep records and compile statistics concerning weather conditions, resource conservation activities, and the number of park visitors.

Many rangers supervise other workers in the parks who build and maintain park facilities, work part-time or seasonally, or operate concession facilities. Rangers often have their own park maintenance responsibilities, such as trail building, landscaping, and caring for visitor centers.

In some parks, rangers are specialists in certain areas of park protection, safety, or management. For example, in areas with heavy snowfalls and a high incidence of avalanches, experts in avalanche control and snow safety are designated *snow rangers*. They monitor snow conditions and patrol park areas to make sure visitors are not lost in snowslides.

Requirements

High School

To prepare for the necessary college courseload you should take courses in earth science, mathematics, English, and speech. Any classes or activities that deal with plant and animal life, the weather, geography, and interacting with others will be helpful.

Postsecondary Training

Employment as a federal or state park ranger requires either a college degree or a specific amount of education and experience. Approximately 200 colleges and universities offer bachelor's degree programs in park management and park recreation. To meet employment requirements, students in other relevant college programs must accumulate at least 24 semester hours of academic credit in park recreation and management, history, behavioral sciences, forestry, botany, geology, or other applicable subject areas.

Without a degree, you will need three years of experience in parks or conservation and must show an understanding of what is required in park work. In addition, you must demonstrate good communications skills. A combination of education and experience can also fulfill job requirements, with one academic year of study equaling nine months of experience. Also, the orientation and training a ranger receives on the job may be supplemented with formal training courses.

Rangers need skills in protecting forests, parks, and wildlife and in interpreting natural or historical resources. Law enforcement and management skills are also important. Rangers who wish to move into management positions may need graduate degrees. Approximately 50 universities offer master's degrees in park recreation and management and 16 have doctoral programs.

Other Requirements

The right kind of person to fill a park ranger position believes in the importance of the country's park resources and the mission of the park system. If you enjoy working outdoors, independently and with others, you may enjoy park ranger work. Rangers need self-confidence, patience, and the ability to stay levelheaded during emergencies. Those who participate in rescues need courage, physical stamina, and endurance, while those who deal with visitors need tact, sincerity, personable natures, and a sense of humor. A sense of camaraderie among fellow rangers also can add to the enjoyment of being a park ranger.

Exploring

If you are interested in exploring park ranger work you may wish to apply for part-time or seasonal work in national, state, or county parks. Such workers usually perform maintenance and other unskilled tasks, but they have opportunities to observe park rangers and talk with them about their work. You might also choose to work as a volunteer. Many park research activities, study projects, and rehabilitation efforts are conducted by volunteer groups affiliated with universities or conservation organizations, and these activities can provide insight into the work done by park rangers.

Employers

Park rangers in the National Park Service are employed by the U.S. Department of the Interior. Other rangers may be employed by other federal agencies or by state and county agencies in charge of their respective parks.

Starting Out

Many workers enter national park ranger jobs after working part time or seasonally at different parks. These workers often work at information desks or in fire control or law enforcement positions. Some help maintain trails, collect trash, or perform forestry activities. Persons interested in applying for park ranger jobs with the federal government should contact their local Federal Job Information Center or the Federal Office of Personnel Management in Washington, DC, for application information. Those people seeking jobs in state parks should write to the appropriate state departments for information.

Advancement

Nearly all rangers start in entry-level positions, which means that nearly all higher-level openings are filled by the promotion of current workers. Entry-level rangers may move into positions as district ranger or park manager, or they may become resource management specialists or park planning specialists. Rangers who show management skills and become park managers may move into administrative positions in the district, regional, or national headquarters.

The orientation and training a ranger receives on the job may be supplemented with formal training courses. Training for job skills unique to the National Park Service is available at the Horace M. Albright Training Center at Grand Canyon National Park in Arizona, and the Stephen T. Mather Training Center at Harpers Ferry, West Virginia. In addition, training is available at the Federal Law Enforcement Training Center in Brunswick, Georgia.

Earnings

Rangers in the National Park Service are usually hired at the GS-5 grade level, with a salary of $21,947 in 2001. More experienced or educated rangers may enter the Park Service at the GS-9 level, which pays $33,254 to start. The government may provide housing to rangers who work in remote areas.

Rangers in state parks work for the state government. They receive comparable salaries and benefits, including paid vacations, sick leave, paid holidays, health and life insurance, and pension plans.

Work Environment

Rangers work in parks all over the country, from the Okefenokee Swamp in Florida to the Rocky Mountains of Colorado. They work in the mountains and forests of Hawaii, Alaska, and California, and in urban and suburban parks throughout the United States.

National park rangers are hired to work 40 hours per week, but their actual working hours can be long and irregular, with a great deal of overtime. They may receive extra pay or time off for working overtime. Some rangers are on call 24 hours a day for emergencies. During the peak tourist seasons, rangers work longer hours. Although many rangers work in offices, many also work outside in all kinds of climates and weather, and most work in a combination of the two settings. Workers may be called upon to risk their own health to rescue injured visitors in cold, snow, rain, and darkness. Rangers in Alaska must adapt to long daylight hours in the summer and short daylight hours in the winter. Working outdoors in beautiful surroundings, however, can be wonderfully stimulating and rewarding for the right kind of worker.

Outlook

Park ranger jobs are scarce, and competition for them is fierce. The U.S. Park Service has reported that the ratio of applicants to available positions is sometimes as high as one hundred to one. As a result, applicants should attain the greatest number and widest variety of applicable skills possible. They may wish to study subjects they can use in other fields: forestry, land management, conservation, wildlife management, history, and natural sciences, for example.

The scarcity of openings is expected to continue indefinitely. Job seekers, therefore, may wish to apply for outdoor work with agencies other than the National Park Service, including other federal land and resource management agencies and similar state and local agencies. Such agencies usually have more openings.

For More Information

For information on federal employment, contact:

Federal Job Information Center
Office of Personnel Management/National Office
1900 E Street, NW, Room 1416
Washington, DC 20415
Tel: 202-606-2700
Web: http://www.usajobs.opm.gov/

For general career information, contact the following organizations:

National Association of State Park Directors
9894 East Holden Place
Tucson, AZ 85748
Tel: 520-298-4924
Email: naspdglen@dakotacom.net
Web: http://www.indiana.edu/~naspd/

National Parks Conservation Association
1300 19th Street, NW, Suite 300
Washington, DC 20036
Email: npca@npca.org
Web: http://www.npca.org/flash.html

National Recreation and Park Association
22377 Belmont Ridge Road
Ashburn, VA 20148-4510
Tel: 703-858-0784
Web: http://www.nrpa.org

Student Conservation Association
PO Box 550
Charlestown, NH 03603-0550
Tel: 603-543-1700
Email: ask-us@sca-inc.org
Web: http://www.sca-inc.org

For information about careers, job openings, and national parks, contact:

U.S. Department of the Interior
National Park Service
1849 C Street, NW
Washington, DC 20240
Tel: 202-208-6843
Web: http://www.nps.gov/

Preschool Teachers

Art English	School Subjects
Communication/ideas Helping/teaching	Personal Skills
Primarily indoors Primarily one location	Work Environment
Some postsecondary training	Minimum Education Level
$12,000 to $17,310 to $30,310	Salary Range
Recommended	Certification or Licensing
Faster than the average	Outlook

Overview

Preschool teachers promote the education of children under age five in all areas. They help students develop physically, socially, and emotionally, work with them on language and communications skills, and help cultivate their cognitive abilities. They also work with families to support parents in raising their young children and reinforcing skills at home. They plan and lead activities developed in accordance with the specific ages and needs of the children. It is the goal of all preschool teachers to help students develop the skills, interests, and individual creativity that they will use for the rest of their lives. Many schools and districts consider kindergarten teachers, who teach students five years of age, to be preschool teachers. For the purposes of this article, *kindergarten teachers* will be included in this category. There are over 380,000 kindergarten and prekindergarten teachers in the United States.

History

Friedrich Froebel, a German educator, founded the first kindergarten ("child's garden" in German) in 1837 in Blankenburg, Germany. He also taught adults how to be kindergarten teachers. One of his adult students, Mrs. Carl Schurz, moved to the United States and started the first kindergarten of this country in Watertown, Wisconsin, in the mid-1800s. By 1873, St. Louis added the first American public kindergarten, and preschools for students under age five began to spring up in Europe around this same time. Preschools were introduced into the United States in the 1920s.

Preschool programs expanded rapidly in the United States during the 1960s, due in large part to the government instituting the Head Start program, designed to help preschool-aged children from low-income families receive educational and socialization opportunities and therefore be better prepared for elementary school. This program also allowed the parents of the children to work during the day. Around the same time, many U.S. public school systems began developing mandatory kindergarten programs for five-year-olds, and today many schools, both preschool and elementary, both public and private, are offering full-day kindergarten programs.

The Job

Preschool teachers plan and lead activities that build on children's abilities and curiosity and aid them in developing skills and characteristics that help them grow. Because children develop at varying skill levels as well as have different temperaments, preschool teachers need to develop a flexible schedule with time allowed for music, art, playtime, academics, rest, and other activities.

Preschool teachers plan activities that encourage children to develop skills appropriate to their developmental needs. For example, they plan activities based on the understanding that a three-year-old child has different motor skills and reasoning abilities than a child of five years of age. They work with the youngest students on learning the days of the week and the recognition of colors, seasons, and animal names and characteristics; they help older students with number and letter recognition and even simple writing skills. Preschool teachers help children with such simple, yet important, tasks as tying shoelaces and washing hands before snack time. Attention to the individual needs of each child is vital; preschool teachers need to be aware of these needs and capabilities, and when possible, adapt activities to the specific needs of the individual child. Self-confidence and the development of communication skills are encouraged in preschools. For example, teachers may give children simple art projects, such as finger painting, and have children show and explain their finished projects to the rest of the class. Show and tell, or "sharing time" as it is often called, gives students opportunities to speak and listen to others.

"A lot of what I teach is based on social skills," says June Gannon, a preschool teacher in Amherst, New Hampshire. "During our circle time, we say hello to one another, sing songs, have show and tell, talk about the weather and do calendar events. We then move on to language arts, which may include talking to children about rules, good listening, helping, sharing, etc., using puppets, work papers, games, and songs."

Preschool teachers adopt many parental responsibilities for the children. They greet the children in the morning and supervise them throughout the day. Often these responsibilities can be quite demanding and complicated. In harsh weather, for example, preschool teachers contend not only with boots, hats, coats, and mittens, but with the inevitable sniffles, colds, and generally cranky behavior that can occur in young children. For most children, preschool is their first time away from home and family for an extended period of time. A major portion of a preschool teacher's day is spent helping children adjust to being away from home and encouraging them to play together. This is especially true at the beginning of the school year. They may need to gently reassure children who become frightened or homesick.

In both full-day and half-day programs, preschool teachers supervise snack time, helping children learn how to eat properly and clean up after themselves. Proper hygiene, such as hand washing before meals, is also stressed. Other activities include storytelling, music, and simple arts and crafts projects. Full-day programs involve a lunch period and at least one nap time. Programs usually have exciting activities interspersed with calmer ones. Even though the children get nap time, preschool teachers must be energetic throughout the day, ready to face with good cheer the many challenges and demands of young children.

Preschool teachers also work with the parents of each child. It is not unusual for parents to come to preschool and observe a child or go on a field trip with the class, and preschool teachers often take these opportunities to discuss the progress of each child as well as any specific problems or concerns. Scheduled meetings are available for parents who cannot visit the school during the day. Solutions to fairly serious problems are worked out in tandem with the parents, often with the aid of the director of the preschool, or in the case of an elementary school kindergarten, with the principal or headmaster.

Kindergarten teachers usually have their own classrooms, made up exclusively of five-year-olds. Although these teachers don't have to plan activities for a wide range of ages, they need to consider individual developmental interests, abilities, and backgrounds represented by the students. Kindergarten teachers usually spend more time helping students with academic skills than do other preschool teachers. While a teacher of a two-, three-, and four-year-old classroom may focus more on socializing and building confidence in students through play and activities, kindergarten teachers often develop activities that help five-year-olds acquire the skills they will need in grade school, such as introductory activities on numbers, reading, and writing.

Requirements

High School

You should take child development, home economics, and other classes that involve you with child care. You'll also need a fundamental understanding of the general subjects you'll be introducing to preschool students, so take English, science, and math. Also, take classes in art, music, and theater to develop creative skills.

Postsecondary Training

Specific education requirements for preschool and kindergarten teachers vary from state to state and also depend on the specific guidelines of the school or district. Many schools and child care centers require preschool teachers to have a bachelor's degree in education or a related field, but others accept adults with a high school diploma and some childcare experience. Some preschool facilities offer on-the-job training to their teachers, hiring them as assistants or aides until they are sufficiently trained to work in a classroom alone. A college degree program should include coursework in a variety of liberal arts subjects, including English, history, and science as well as nutrition, child development, psychology of the young child, and sociology.

Several groups offer on-the-job training programs for prospective preschool teachers. For example, the American Montessori Society offers a career program for aspiring preschool teachers. This program requires a three-month classroom training period followed by one year of supervised on-the-job training.

Certification or Licensing

In some states, licensure may be required. Many states accept the Child Development Associate credential or an associate or bachelor's degree as sufficient requirements for work in a preschool facility. Individual state boards of education can provide specific licensure information. Kindergarten teachers working in public elementary schools almost always need teaching certification similar to that required by other elementary school teachers in the school. Other types of licensure or certification may be required, depending upon the school or district. These may include first-aid or cardiopulmonary resuscitation (CPR) training.

Other Requirements

Because young children look up to adults and learn through example, it is especially important that a preschool teacher be a good role model. "Remember how important your job is," June Gannon says. "Everything you say and do will affect these children." Gannon also emphasizes being respectful of the children and keeping a sense of humor. "I have patience and lots of heart for children," she says. "You definitely need both."

Exploring

Preschools, daycare centers, and other childcare programs often hire high school students for part-time positions as aides. There are also many volunteer opportunities for working with kids. Check with your library or local literacy program about tutoring children and reading to preschoolers. Summer day camps or Bible schools with preschool classes also hire high school students as counselors or counselors-in-training. Discussing the field with preschool teachers and observing in their classes are other good ways to discover specific job information and explore one's aptitude for this career.

Employers

Six of every 10 mothers of children under the age of six are in the labor force, and the number is rising. Both government and the private sector are working to fill the enormous need for quality childcare. Preschool teachers will find many job opportunities in private and public preschools, including daycare centers, government-funded learning programs, churches, and Montessori schools. They may find work in a small center, or with a large preschool with many students and classrooms. Preschool franchises, like Primrose Schools and Kids 'R' Kids International, are also providing more opportunities for preschool teachers.

Starting Out

Before becoming a preschool teacher, June Gannon gained a lot of experience in child care. "I have worked as a special education aide and have taken numerous classes in childhood education," she says. "I am a sign language interpreter and have taught deaf children in a public school inclusion program."

Aspiring preschool teachers can contact child care centers, nursery schools, Head Start programs, and other preschool facilities to identify job opportunities. Often jobs for preschool teachers are listed in the classified section of newspapers. In addition, many school districts and state boards of education maintain job listings of available teaching positions. If no permanent positions are available at preschools, new graduates may be able to find opportunities to work as a substitute teacher. Most preschools and kindergartens maintain a substitute list and refer to it frequently.

Advancement

Many teachers advance by becoming more skillful in what they do. Skilled preschool teachers, especially those with additional training, usually receive salary increases as they become more experienced. A few preschool teachers with administrative ability and an interest in administrative work advance to the position of director. Administrators need to have at least a master's degree in child development or a related field and have to meet any state or federal licensing regulations. Some become directors of Head Start programs or other government programs. A relatively small number of experienced preschool teachers open their own facilities. This entails not only the ability to be an effective administrator but also the knowledge of how to operate a business. Kindergarten teachers sometimes have the opportunity to earn more money by teaching at a higher grade level in the elementary school. This salary increase is especially true when a teacher moves from a half-day kindergarten program to a full-day grade school classroom.

Earnings

Although there have been some attempts to correct the discrepancies in salaries between preschool teachers and other teachers, salaries in this profession tend to be lower than teaching positions in public elementary and high schools. Because some preschool programs are only in the morning or afternoon, many preschool teachers work only part time. As part-time workers, they often do not receive medical insurance or other benefits and may get paid minimum wage to start.

According to the U.S. Bureau of Labor Statistics, preschool teachers earned a median salary of about $17,310 a year in 1998. The lowest 10 percent earned less than $12,000, while the highest 10 percent earned more than $30,310. Kindergarten teachers, on average, have the highest salaries in this field, earning about the same as elementary school teachers (a median of $23,300 in 1997). A 1997 report from the National Education Association estimated the annual average teacher salary to be $38,611.

Work Environment

Preschool teachers spend much of their work day on their feet in a classroom or on a playground. Facilities vary from a single room to large buildings. Class sizes also vary; some preschools serve only a handful of children, while others serve several hundred. Classrooms may be crowded and noisy, but anyone who loves children will enjoy all the activity. "The best part about working with children," June Gannon says, "is the laughter, the fun, the enjoyment of watching the children grow physically, emotionally, and intellectually."

Many children do not go to preschool all day, so work may be part-time. Part-time employees generally work between 18 and 30 hours a week, while full-time employees work 35 to 40 hours a week. Part-time work gives the employee flexibility, and for many, this is one of the advantages of the job. Some preschool teachers teach both morning and afternoon classes, going through the same schedule and lesson plans with two sets of students.

Outlook

Employment opportunities for preschool teachers are expected to increase faster than the average for all occupations through 2008, according to the U.S. Department of Labor. Specific job opportunities vary from state to state and depend on demographic characteristics and level of government funding. Jobs should be available at private child care centers, nursery schools, Head Start facilities, public and private kindergartens, and laboratory schools connected with universities and colleges. In the past, the majority of preschool teachers were female, and although this continues to be the case, more males are becoming involved in early childhood education.

One-third of all childcare workers leave their centers each year, often because of the low pay and lack of benefits. This will mean plenty of job openings for preschool teachers and possibly improved benefit plans, as centers attempt to maintain qualified preschool teachers.

For More Information

For information on training programs, contact:

American Montessori Society
281 Park Avenue South, 6th Floor
New York, NY 10010-6102
Tel: 212-358-1250
Web: http://www.amshq.org

For information about certification, contact:

Council for Professional Recognition
2460 16th Street, NW
Washington, DC 20009-3575
Tel: 800-424-4310
Web: http://www.cdacouncil.org

For general information on preschool teaching careers, contact:

National Association for the Education of Young Children
1509 16th Street, NW
Washington, DC 20036-1426
Tel: 800-424-2460
Email: naeyc@naeyc.org
Web: http://www.naeyc.org

For information about student memberships and training opportunities, contact:

National Association of Child Care Professionals
PO Box 90723
Austin, TX 78709-0723
Tel: 512-301-5557
Email: admin@naccp.org
Web: http://www.naccp.org

School Administrators

Business English	School Subjects
Helping/teaching Leadership/management	Personal Skills
Primarily indoors Primarily one location	Work Environment
Master's degree	Minimum Education Level
$30,480 to $60,400 to $130,000	Salary Range
Required by all states	Certification or Licensing
As fast as the average	Outlook

Overview

School administrators are leaders who plan and set goals related to the educational, administrative, and counseling programs of schools. They coordinate and evaluate the activities of teachers and other school personnel to ensure that they adhere to deadlines and budget requirements and meet established objectives.

History

The history of school administrators is almost as old as the history of education itself. The first American colonists of the 17th century set up schools in their homes. In the 18th century, groups of prosperous parents established separate schools and employed schoolmasters. In these small early schools, the teachers were also the administrators, charged with the operation of the school as well as with the instruction of the pupils.

In the early 1800s, the importance of education gained recognition among people from all classes of society and the government became involved in providing schooling without cost to all children. Schools grew larger, a more complex system of education evolved, and there developed a demand for educators specializing in the area of administration.

In the United States, each state has its own school system, headed by a *superintendent* or *commissioner of education* who works in conjunction with the state board of education. The states are divided into local school districts, which may vary in size from a large urban area to a sparsely populated area containing a single classroom of children. The board of education in each district elects a professionally trained superintendent or *supervising principal* to administer the local schools. In most school districts the superintendent has one or more *assistants,* and in a very large district the superintendent may also be assisted by *business managers, directors of curriculum,* or *research and testing personnel.* Individual schools within a district are usually headed by a *school principal*, with one or more *assistant principals.* The administrative staff of a very large secondary school may also include deans, registrars, department heads, counselors, and others.

The problems of school administrators today are much more complex than in the past and require political as well as administrative skills. School leaders are confronted by such volatile issues as desegregation, school closings and reduced enrollments, contract negotiations with teachers, student and staff safety, and greatly increased costs coupled with public resistance to higher taxes.

The Job

The occupation of school administrator includes school district superintendents, assistant superintendents, school principals, and assistant principals. Private schools also have administrators, often known as *school directors* or *headmasters.* Administrators in either public or private schools are responsible for the smooth, efficient operation of an individual school or an entire school system, depending on the size and type of the school or the size of the district. They make plans, set goals, and supervise and coordinate the activities of teachers and other school personnel in carrying out those plans within the established time framework and budget allowance. The general job descriptions that follow refer to administrators in the public school system.

School principals far outnumber the other school administrators and are the most familiar to the students, who often think of them as disciplinarians. Principals spend a great deal of time resolving conflicts that students and teachers may have with one another, with parents, or with school board policies, but their authority extends to many other matters. They are responsible for the performance of an individual school, directing and coordinating educational, administrative, and counseling activities according to standards set by the superintendent and the board of education. They hire and assign teachers and other staff, help them improve their skills, and evaluate their performance. They plan and evaluate the instructional programs jointly with teachers. Periodically, they visit classrooms to observe the effectiveness of the teachers and teaching methods, review educational objectives, and examine learning materials, always seeking ways to improve the quality of instruction.

Principals are responsible for the registration, schedules, and attendance of pupils. In cases of severe educational or behavioral problems, they may confer with teachers, students, parents, and counselors and recommend corrective measures. They cooperate with community organizations, colleges, and other schools to coordinate educational services. They oversee the day-to-day operations of the school building and requisition and allocate equipment, supplies, and instructional materials.

A school principal's duties necessitate a great deal of paperwork: filling out forms, preparing administrative reports, and keeping records. They also spend much of each day meeting with people: teachers and other school personnel, colleagues, students, parents, and other members of the community.

In larger schools, usually secondary schools, principals may have one or more assistants. Assistant principals, who may be known as *deans of students,* provide counseling for individuals or student groups related to personal problems, educational or vocational objectives, and social and recreational activities. They often handle discipline, interviewing students, and taking whatever action is necessary in matters such as truancy and delinquency. Assistant principals generally plan and supervise social and recreational programs and coordinate other school activities.

Superintendents manage the affairs of an entire school district, which may range in size from a small town with a handful of schools to a city with a population of millions. Superintendents must be elected by the board of education to oversee and coordinate the activities of all the schools in the district in accordance with board of education standards. They select and employ staff and negotiate contracts. They develop and administer budgets, the acquisition and maintenance of school buildings, and the purchase and distribution of school supplies and equipment. They coordinate related activities with other school districts and agencies. They speak before community and civic groups and try to enlist their support. In addition, they collect statistics, prepare reports, enforce compulsory attendance, and oversee the operation of the school transportation system and provision of health services.

School district superintendents usually have one or more assistants or deputies, whose duties vary depending on the size and nature of the school system. Assistant superintendents may have charge of a particular geographic area or may specialize in activities pertaining, for example, to budget, personnel, or curriculum development.

Boards of education vary in their level of authority and their method of appointment or election to the post of board member. Normally, board members are elected from leaders in the community in business and education. It is not uncommon to have the board selected by the mayor or other city administrator.

Requirements

High School

School administration calls for a high level of education and experience. For this reason, you should begin preparing for the job by taking a wide range of college preparatory courses, including English, mathematics, science, music, art, history, and computers. A broad secondary school education will help you as you pursue your college degrees and gain admittance into strong colleges of education.

Postsecondary Training

Principals and assistant principals are generally required to have a master's degree in educational administration in addition to several years' experience as a classroom teacher.

School superintendents usually must have had graduate training in educational administration, preferably at the doctoral level. Some larger districts require a law degree or a business degree in addition to a graduate degree in education. Candidates for the position of school superintendent generally must have accumulated previous experience as an administrator.

Around 250 universities offer graduate programs in educational administration accredited by the National Council for Accreditation of Teacher Education. Programs are designed specifically for elementary school principals, secondary school principals, or school district superintendents and include such courses as school management, school law, curriculum development and evaluation, and personnel administration. A semester of internship and field experience are extremely valuable.

Certification or Licensing

Licensure of school administrators is mandatory in all 50 states and the District of Columbia. Requirements to become licensed may include U.S. citizenship or state residency, graduate training in educational administration, experience, and good health and character. In some states, candidates must pass a qualifying examination. You can obtain information on specific requirements from the department of education in your state.

Other Requirements

You should have leadership skills necessary for keeping the school operating smoothly. You also need good communication skills and the ability to get along with many different types and ages of people. Strong self-motivation and self-confidence are important for putting your plans into action, and for withstanding criticism.

Exploring

If you've been attending a private or public school, you're already very familiar with the nature of education, and already know many great resources of information, such as your own teachers and school administrators. Talk to your teachers about their work, and offer to assist them with some projects before or after school. School counselors can offer vocational guidance, provide occupational materials, and help students plan appropriate programs of study.

You can gain experience in the education field by teaching Sunday school classes, getting summer jobs as camp counselors or day care center aides, working with a scouting group, volunteering to coach a youth athletic team, or tutoring younger students.

Employers

Principals work in either public or private schools at the elementary or secondary level. Superintendents work for a school district, which may include many elementary and secondary schools. School administrators are also needed for large preschools and job training programs. See the chapter on College Administrators to learn about opportunities with colleges and universities.

Starting Out

Most school administrators enter the field as teachers. College and university placement offices may help place you in your first teaching job, or you may apply directly to a local school system. Teachers, of course, must meet the requirements for state licensure. Many school districts and state departments of education maintain job listings that notify potential teachers and administrators of openings. Qualified candidates may also come from other administrative jobs, such as curriculum specialist, financial advisor, or director of audiovisual aids, libraries, arts, or special education. The important thing is having experience in organizing and supervising school programs and activities.

Advancement

A teacher may be promoted directly to principal, but more often teachers begin as assistant principals and in time are promoted. Experienced administrators may advance to assistant superintendent and then superintendent. In fact, many school superintendents are former principals who worked their way up the administrative ladder. Each increase in responsibility usually carries a corresponding salary increase.

Earnings

The income of school administrators depends on the position, the level of responsibility, and the size and geographic location of the school or school district. The highest salaries are paid in the far western and mid-Atlantic states; the lowest, in the Southeast.

The *Occupational Outlook Handbook* reports that median annual earnings of education administrators in 1998 were $60,400 a year. Salaries ranged from less than $30,480 to more than $92,680.

The Educational Research Service conducted a survey of the salaries of public school administrators for the 1997-98 school year. Assistant principals earned an average of $53,206 a year in elementary schools, and $60,999 a year in high schools. Elementary school principals made about $64,653 a year, while high school principals made $74,380. The average annual salary for a deputy superintendent was $98,617. Superintendents earned annual salaries of $106,122. Superintendents of large school districts (25,000 or more pupils) can make more than $130,000 a year.

School administrators also receive a variety of other benefits including health insurance, retirement plans, and vacation and sick leave.

Work Environment

School administrators work a standard 40-hour week, although they often attend meetings or handle urgent matters in the evenings or on weekends. The job requires year-round attention, even during school vacations.

Administrators work in pleasant office environments, usually at a desk. At times, however, they attend meetings elsewhere with PTA members, the school board, and civic groups. Principals and their assistants periodically sit in on classes, attend school assemblies and sporting events, and conduct inspections of the school's physical facilities.

Outlook

The American Association of School Administrators (AASA) reports that 6,000 school superintendents will need to be replaced over the next five years because half of them are expected to leave or retire in that time. There is a shortage of qualified candidates to fill those positions. One issue is education: more than half (54 percent) of working superintendents don't have doctoral degrees, but many school boards prefer candidates with doctorates. Other issues include the perception that school administration is too political, low pay, and constraints on moving between districts.

According to AASA, a new career is developing to handle the shortage. A number of districts have hired interim superintendents as temporary replacements until a permanent candidate can be found.

The number of school administrators employed is determined to a large extent by state and local expenditures for education. Budget cuts not only affect the number of available positions in administration, but also affect how an administrator can perform his or her job. Administrators in the coming years will have to remain creative in finding funds for their schools. School administrators are also faced with developing additional programs for children as more parents work outside the home. Schools may be expected to help care for children before and after regular school hours.

Administrators may also be overseeing smaller learning environments in the coming years. Research has proven that smaller classrooms and more individual attention not only improve education, but help educators identify students with personal and emotional problems. In order to keep students safe from violence, drug abuse, and street gangs, administrators may be called upon to develop more individualized education.

For More Information

For articles and news reports about the career of school administrator, contact the following organizations:

American Association of School Administrators
1801 North Moore Street
Arlington, VA 22209
Tel: 703-528-0700
Web: http://www.aasa.org

National Association of Elementary School Principals
1615 Duke Street
Alexandria, VA 22314
Tel: 703-684-3345
Web: http://www.naesp.org

National Association of Secondary School Principals
1904 Association Drive
Reston, VA 20191
Tel: 703-860-0200
Web: http://www.nassp.org

Secondary School Teachers

School Subjects	English Psychology
Personal Skills	Communication/ideas Helping/teaching
Work Environment	Primarily indoors Primarily one location
Minimum Education Level	Bachelor's degree
Salary Range	$19,000 to $35,000 to $70,000
Certification or Licensing	Required by all states
Outlook	Faster than the average

Overview

Secondary school teachers teach students in grades seven through 12. Specializing in one subject area, such as English or math, these teachers work with five or more groups of students during the day. They lecture, direct discussions, and test students' knowledge with exams, essays, and homework assignments.

History

Early secondary education was typically based upon training students to enter the clergy. Benjamin Franklin pioneered the idea of a broader secondary education with the creation of the academy, which offered a flexible curriculum and a wide variety of academic subjects.

It was not until the 19th century, however, that children of different social classes commonly attended school into the secondary grades. The first English Classical School, which was to become the model for public high schools throughout the country, was established in 1821, in Boston. An adjunct to the high school, the junior high school, was conceived by Dr. Charles W. Eliot, president of Harvard. In a speech before the National Education Association in 1888, he recommended that secondary studies be started two years earlier than was then the custom. The first such school opened in 1908, in Columbus, Ohio. Another opened a year later in Berkeley, California. By the early 20th century, secondary school attendance was made mandatory in the United States.

The Job

Many successful people credit secondary school teachers with helping guide them into college, careers, and other endeavors. Students may look to secondary school teachers for help in a number of areas. Their primary responsibility to their students in grades seven through 12 is to educate them in a specific subject. But they also inform students about colleges, occupations, and such varied subjects as the arts, health, and relationships. Secondary school teachers may teach in a traditional area, such as science, English, history, and math, or they may teach more specialized classes, such as information technology, business, and theater. Many secondary schools are expanding their course offerings to better serve the individual interests of their students. "School-to-work" programs, which are vocational education programs designed for high school students and recent graduates, involve lab work and demonstrations to prepare students for highly technical jobs. Though they will likely be assigned to one specific level in your subject area, secondary school teachers may be required to teach multiple levels. For example, a secondary school mathematics teacher may teach algebra to a class of ninth-graders one period and trigonometry to high school seniors the next.

In the classroom, secondary school teachers rely on a variety of teaching methods. They spend a great deal of time lecturing, but they also facilitate student discussion and develop projects and activities to interest the students in the subject. They show films and videos, use computers and the Internet, and bring in guest speakers. They assign essays, presentations, and other projects. Each individual subject calls upon particular approaches, and may involve laboratory experiments, role-playing exercises, shop work, and field trips.

Outside of the classroom, secondary school teachers prepare lectures, lesson plans, and exams. They evaluate student work and calculate grades. In the process of planning their class, secondary school teachers read textbooks, novels, and workbooks to determine reading assignments; photocopy notes, articles, and other handouts; and develop grading policies. They also continue to study alternative and traditional teaching methods to hone their skills. They prepare students for special events and conferences and submit student work to competitions. Many secondary school teachers also serve as sponsors to student organizations in their field. For example, a *French teacher* may sponsor the French club and a *journalism teacher* may advise the yearbook staff. Some secondary school teachers also have the opportunity for extracurricular work as athletic coaches or drama coaches. Teachers also monitor students during lunch or break times, and sit in on study halls. They may also accompany student groups on field days, and to competitions and events. Some teachers also have the opportunity to escort students on educational vacations to foreign countries, and to Washington, DC, and other major U.S. cities. Secondary school teachers attend faculty meetings, meetings with parents, and state and national teacher conferences.

Some teachers explore their subject area outside of the requirements of the job. *English and writing teachers* may publish in magazines and journals; *business and technology teachers* may have small businesses of their own; *music teachers* may perform and record their music; *art teachers* may show work in galleries; *sign-language teachers* may do freelance interpreting.

Requirements

High School

You should follow your guidance counselor's college preparatory program and take advanced classes in such subjects as English, science, math, and government. You should also explore an extracurricular activity, such as theater, sports, and debate, so that you can offer these additional skills to future employers. If you're already aware of which subject you'd like to teach, take all the courses in that area that are available. You should also take speech and composition courses to develop your communication skills.

Postsecondary Training

There are over 500 accredited teacher education programs in the United States. Most of these programs are designed to meet the certification requirements for the state in which they're located. Some states may require that you pass a test before being admitted to an education program. You may choose to major in your subject area while taking required education courses, or you may major in secondary education with a concentration in your subject area. You'll probably have advisors in both colleges to help you select courses. Practice teaching, also called student teaching, in an actual school situation is usually required. The student is placed in a school to work with a full-time teacher. During the period of practice teaching, the undergraduate student will observe the ways in which lessons are presented and the classroom is managed, learn how to keep records of such details as attendance and grades, and get actual experience in handling the class, both under supervision and alone. Besides licensure and courses in education, prospective high school teachers usually need 24 to 36 hours of college work in the subject they wish to teach. Some states require a master's degree; teachers with master's degrees can earn higher salaries. Private schools generally do not require an education degree.

Certification or Licensing

Public school teachers must be licensed under regulations established by the department of education of the state in which they are teaching. Not all states require licensure for teachers in private or parochial schools. When you've received your teaching degree, you may request that a transcript of your college record be sent to the licensure section of the state department of education. If you have met licensure requirements, you will receive a certificate and thus be eligible to teach in the public schools of the state. In some states, you may have to take additional tests. If you move to another state, you will have to resubmit college transcripts, as well as comply with any other regulations in the new state to be able to teach there.

Other Requirements

You'll need respect for young people, and a genuine interest in their success in life. You'll also need patience. Adolescence can be a troubling time for children, and these troubles often affect behavior and classroom performance. You'll also be working with students who are at very impressionable ages; you should serve as a good role model. You should also be well organized, as you'll have to keep track of the work and progress of a number of different students.

Exploring

By attending your high school classes, you've already gained a good sense of the daily work of a secondary school teacher. But the requirements of a teacher extend far beyond the classroom, so ask to spend some time with one of your teachers after school, and ask to look at lecture notes and record-keeping procedures. Interview your teachers about the amount of work that goes into preparing a class and directing an extracurricular activity. To get some firsthand teaching experience, volunteer for a peer tutoring program. Many other teaching opportunities may exist in your community. Look into coaching an athletic team at the YMCA, counseling at a summer camp, teaching an art course at a community center, or assisting with a community theater production.

Employers

Secondary school teachers are needed at public and private schools, including parochial schools, juvenile detention centers, vocational schools, and schools of the arts. Some Montessori schools are also expanding to include high school courses. Secondary school teachers work in middle schools, junior high schools, and high schools. Though some rural areas maintain schools, most secondary schools are in towns and cities of all sizes. Teachers are also finding opportunities in "charter" schools, which are smaller, deregulated schools that receive public funding.

Starting Out

After completing the teacher certification process, including your months of student teaching, you'll work with your college's placement office to find a full-time position. The departments of education of some states maintain listings of job openings. Many schools advertise teaching positions in the classifieds of the state's major newspapers. You may also directly contact the principals and superintendents of the schools in which you'd like to work. While waiting for full-time work, you can work as a substitute teacher. In urban areas with many schools, you may be able to substitute full-time.

Advancement

Most teachers advance in the sense that they become more expert in the job that they have chosen. There is usually an increase in salary as teachers acquire experience. Additional training or study can also bring an increase in salary.

A few teachers with administrative ability and interest in administrative work may advance to the position of *principal*. Others may work into supervisory positions, and some may become helping teachers who are charged with the responsibility of helping other teachers find appropriate instructional materials and develop certain phases of their courses of study. Others may go into teacher education at a college or university. For most of these positions, additional education is required. Some teachers also make lateral moves into other education-related positions such as guidance counselor or resource room teacher.

Earnings

Most teachers are contracted to work nine months out of the year, though some contracts are made for 10 or a full 12 months. (When regular school is not in session, teachers are expected to conduct summer teaching, planning, or other school-related work.) In most cases, teachers have the option of prorating their salary up to 52 weeks.

According to the U.S. Department of Labor, the median annual salary for kindergarten, elementary, and secondary school teachers was between $33,590 to $37,890 in 1998. The lowest 10 percent earned between $19,710 and $24,390; the highest 10 percent earned between $53,720 and $70,030.

The American Federation of Teachers released survey results in 1999. This report found that the average beginning salary for a teacher with only a bachelor's degree was $26,639. The average maximum salary for a teacher with a master's degree was $47,439.

Teachers can also supplement their earnings through teaching summer classes, coaching sports, sponsoring a club, or other extracurricular work.

On behalf of the teachers, unions bargain with schools over contract conditions such as wages, hours, and benefits. Most teachers join the American Federation of Teachers or the National Education Association. Depending on the state, teachers usually receive a retirement plan, sick leave, and health and life insurance. Some systems grant teachers sabbatical leave.

Work Environment

Although the job of the secondary school teacher is not overly strenuous, it can be tiring and trying. Secondary school teachers must stand for many hours each day, do a lot of talking, show energy and enthusiasm, and handle discipline problems. But they also have the reward of guiding their students as they make decisions about their lives and futures.

Secondary school teachers work under generally pleasant conditions, though some older schools may have poor heating and electrical systems. Though violence in schools has decreased in recent years, media coverage of the violence has increased, along with student fears. In most schools, students are prepared to learn and to perform the work that's required of them. But in some schools, students may be dealing with gangs, drugs, poverty, and other problems, so the environment can be tense and emotional.

School hours are generally 8 AM to 3 PM, but teachers work more than 40 hours a week teaching, preparing for classes, grading papers, and directing extracurricular activities. As a coach, or as a music or drama director, teachers may have to work some evenings and weekends. Many teachers enroll in master's or doctoral programs and take evening and summer courses to continue their education.

Outlook

The U.S. Department of Education predicts that 322,000 more secondary teachers will be needed by 2008 to meet rising enrollments and to replace the large number of retiring teachers. The National Education Association believes this will be a challenge because of the low salaries that are paid to secondary school teachers. Higher salaries will be necessary to attract new teachers and retain experienced ones, along with other changes such as smaller classroom sizes and safer schools. Other challenges for the profession involve attracting more men into teaching. The percentage of male teachers at this level continues to decline.

In order to improve education for all children, changes are being considered by some districts. Some private companies are managing public schools. Though it is believed that a private company can afford to provide better facilities, faculty, and equipment, this hasn't been proven. Teacher organizations are concerned about taking school management away from communities and turning it over to remote corporate headquarters. Charter schools and voucher programs are two other controversial alternatives to traditional public education. Charter schools, which are small schools that are publicly funded but not guided by the rules and regulations of traditional public schools, are viewed by some as places of innovation and improved educational methods; others see charter schools as ill-equipped and unfairly funded with money that could better benefit local school districts. Vouchers, which exist only in a few cities, allow students to attend private schools courtesy of tuition vouchers; these vouchers are paid for with public tax dollars. In theory, the vouchers allow for more choices in education for poor and minority students, but private schools still have the option of being highly selective in their admissions. Teacher organizations see some danger in giving public funds to unregulated private schools.

For More Information

For information about careers and issues affecting teachers, contact or visit the Web sites of the following organizations:

American Federation of Teachers
555 New Jersey Avenue, NW
Washington, DC 20001
Tel: 202-879-4400
Email: online@aft.org
Web: http://www.aft.org

National Education Association
1201 16th Street, NW
Washington, DC 20036
Tel: 202-833-4000
Web: http://www.nea.org

For information on accredited training programs, contact:

National Council for Accreditation of Teacher Education
2010 Massachusetts Avenue, NW, Suite 500
Washington, DC 20036-1023
Tel: 202-466-7496
Email: ncate@ncate.org
Web: http://www.ncate.org

Special Education Teachers

English Speech	School Subjects
Communication/ideas Helping/teaching	Personal Skills
Primarily indoors Primarily one location	Work Environment
Bachelor's degree	Minimum Education Level
$25,450 to $37,850 to $78,030+	Salary Range
Required by all states	Certification or Licensing
Faster than the average	Outlook

Overview

Special education teachers teach students, aged three through 21, with a variety of disabilities. They design individualized education plans and work with students one-on-one to help them learn academic subjects and life skills.

The Job

Special education teachers instruct students who have a variety of disabilities. Their students may have physical disabilities, such as vision, hearing, or orthopedic impairment. They may also have learning disabilities or serious emotional disturbances. Although less common, special education teachers sometimes work with students who are gifted and talented, children who have limited proficiency in English, children who have communicable diseases, or children who are neglected and abused.

In order to teach special education students, these teachers design and modify instruction so that it is tailored to individual student needs. Teachers collaborate with school psychologists, social workers, parents, and occupational, physical, and speech-language therapists to develop a specially-designed program called an Individualized Education Program (IEP) for each one of their students. The IEP sets personalized goals for a student, based upon his or her learning style and ability, and outlines specific steps to prepare him or her for employment or postsecondary schooling.

Special education teachers teach at a pace that is dictated by the individual needs and abilities of their students. Unlike most regular classes, special education classes do not have an established curriculum that is taught to all students at the same time. Because student abilities vary widely, instruction is individualized and it is part of the teacher's responsibility to match specific techniques with a student's learning style and abilities. They may spend much time working with students one-on-one or in small groups.

Working with different types of students requires a variety of teaching methods. Some students may need to use special equipment or skills in the classroom in order to overcome their disabilities. For example, a teacher working with a student with a physical disability might use a computer that is operated by touching a screen or by voice commands. To work with hearing-impaired students, the teacher may need to use sign language. With visually impaired students, he or she may use teaching materials that have Braille characters or large, easy-to-see type. Gifted and talented students may need extra challenging assignments, a faster learning pace, or special attention in one curriculum area, such as art or music.

In addition to teaching academic subjects, special education teachers help students develop both emotionally and socially. They work to make students as independent as possible by teaching them functional skills for daily living. They may help young children learn basic grooming, hygiene, and table manners. Older students might be taught how to balance a checkbook, follow a recipe, or use the public transportation system.

Special education teachers meet regularly with their students' parents to inform them of their child's progress and offer suggestions of how to promote learning at home. They may also meet with school administrators, social workers, psychologists, various types of therapists, and students' general education teachers.

The current trend in education is to integrate students with disabilities into regular classrooms to the extent that it is possible and beneficial to them. This is often called "mainstreaming." As mainstreaming becomes increasingly common, special education teachers frequently work with general education teachers in general education classrooms. They may help adapt curriculum materials and teaching techniques to meet the needs of students with disabilities and offer guidance on dealing with students' emotional and behavioral problems.

In addition to working with students, special education teachers are responsible for a certain amount of paperwork. They document each student's progress and may fill out any forms that are required by the school system or the government.

Requirements

High School

High school students who are considering a career as a special education teacher should focus on courses that will prepare them for college. These classes include natural and social sciences, mathematics, and English. Speech classes would also be a good choice for improving one's communication skills. Finally, classes in psychology might be helpful both to help prospective teachers understand the students they will eventually teach, and prepare them for college-level psychology course work.

Postsecondary Training

All states require that teachers have at least a bachelor's degree and that they complete a prescribed number of subject and education credits. It is increasingly common for special education teachers to complete an additional fifth year of training after they receive their bachelor's degree. Many states require special education teachers to get a master's degree in special education.

There are approximately 700 colleges and universities in the United States that offer programs in special education, including undergraduate, master's, and doctoral programs. These programs include general and specialized courses in special education, including educational psychology, legal issues of special education, child growth and development, and knowledge and skills needed for teaching students with disabilities. The student typically spends the last year of the program student-teaching in an actual classroom, under the supervision of a licensed teacher.

Certification or Licensing

All states also require that special education teachers be licensed, although the particulars of licensing vary by state. In some states, these teachers must first be certified as elementary or secondary school teachers, then meet specific requirements to teach special education. Some states offer general special education licensure; others license several different subspecialties within special education. Some states allow special education teachers to transfer their license from one state to another, but many still require these teachers to pass licensing requirements for that state.

Other Requirements

Special education teachers need to have many of the same personal characteristics as regular classroom teachers: the ability to communicate, a broad knowledge of the arts, sciences, and history, and a love of children. In addition, these teachers need a great deal of patience and persistence. They need to be creative, flexible, cooperative, and accepting of differences in others. Finally, they need to be emotionally stable and consistent in their dealings with students.

Exploring

There are a number of ways for the interested high school student to explore the field of special education. One of the first and easiest might be to approach a special education teacher at his or her school and ask to talk about the job. Perhaps the teacher could provide a tour of the special education classroom, or allow the student to visit while a class is in session.

Students might also become acquainted with special-needs students at their school, or become involved in a school or community mentoring program for these students. There may also be other opportunities for volunteer work or part-time jobs in the school, community agencies, camps, or residential facilities that allow students to work with persons with disabilities.

Employers

The majority of special education teachers work in public school systems. The next largest group are employed by local education agencies, and a minority of others work in colleges and universities, private schools, and state education agencies.

Starting Out

Because public school systems are by far the largest employers of special education teachers, this is where you should focus your job search.

Since you must have at least a bachelor's degree to teach special education, you should have access to your college's career placement center. This may prove a very effective place to begin. You may also write to your state department of education for information on placement and regulations, or contact state employment offices to enquire about job openings. Applying directly to local school systems can sometimes be effective. Even if a school system does not have an immediate opening, it will usually keep applicant resumes on file, should a vacancy occur.

Advancement

Advancement opportunities for special education teachers, as for regular classroom teachers, are fairly limited. They may take the form of higher wages, better facilities, or more prestige. In some cases, these teachers do advance to become supervisors or administrators, although this may require continued education on the teacher's part. Another option is for special education teachers to earn advanced degrees and become instructors at the college level.

Earnings

In some school districts, salaries for special education teachers follow the same scale as general education teachers. The average salary for special education teachers is $37,850, according to the *Occupational Outlook Handbook*. The lowest 10 percent earned less than $25,450, while the highest 10 percent earned more than $78,030. Public secondary schools paid an average of $39,000; elementary schools, $38,000. Private school teachers usually earn less as compared with their public school counterparts. Teachers can supplement their annual salaries by becoming an activity sponsor, or by summer work.

Other school districts pay their special education teachers on a separate scale, which is usually higher than that of general education teachers.

Regardless of the salary scale, special education teachers usually receive a complete benefits package, which includes health and life insurance, paid holidays and vacations, and a pension plan.

Work Environment

The special education teacher usually works from 7:30 or 8 AM to 3 or 3:30 PM. Like most teachers, however, he or she typically spends several hours in the evening grading papers, completing paperwork, or preparing lessons for the next day. Altogether, most special education teachers work more than the standard 40 hours per week.

Although some schools offer year-round classes for students, the majority of special education teachers work the traditional 10-month school year, with a two-month vacation in the summer. Many teachers find this work schedule very appealing, as it gives them the opportunity to pursue personal interests or additional education during the summer break. Teachers typically also get a week off at Christmas and for spring break.

Special education teachers work in a variety of settings in schools, including both ordinary and specially equipped classrooms, resource rooms, and therapy rooms. Some schools have newer and better facilities for special education than others. Although it is less common, some teachers work in residential facilities or tutor students who are homebound or hospitalized.

Working with special education students can be very demanding, due to their physical and emotional needs. Teachers may fight a constant battle to keep certain students, particularly those with behavior disorders, under control. Other students, such as those with mental impairments or learning disabilities, learn so slowly that it may seem as if they are making no progress. The special education teacher must deal daily with frustration, setbacks, and classroom disturbances.

These teachers must also contend with heavy workloads, including a great deal of paperwork to document each student's progress. In addition, they may sometimes be faced with irate parents who feel that their child is not receiving proper treatment or an adequate education.

The positive side of this job is in helping students overcome their disabilities and learn to be as functional as possible. For a special education teacher, knowing that he or she is making a difference in a child's life can be very rewarding and emotionally fulfilling.

Outlook

The field of special education is expected to grow faster than the average through 2008, according to the U.S. Department of Labor. This demand is caused partly by the growth in the number of special education students needing services. Medical advances resulting in more survivors of illness and accidents, the rise in birth defects, especially in older pregnancies, as well as general population growth, are also significant factors for strong demand. Because of the rise in the number of youths with disabilities under the age of 21, the government has given approval for more federally funded programs. Growth of jobs in this field has also been influenced positively by legislation emphasizing training and employment for individuals with disabilities and a growing public awareness and interest in those with disabilities.

Finally, there is a fairly high turnover rate in this field, as special education teachers find the work too stressful and switch to mainstream teaching or change jobs altogether. Many job openings will arise out of a need to replace teachers who have left their positions. There is a shortage of qualified teachers in rural areas and in the inner city. Jobs will also be plentiful for teachers who specialize in speech and language impairments, learning disabilities, and early childhood intervention. Bilingual teachers with multicultural experience will be in high demand.

For More Information

For information on current issues, legal cases, and conferences, contact:

Council of Administrators of Special Education
615 16th Street, NW
Albuquerque, NM 87104
Tel: 505-243-7622
Web: http://members.aol.com/casecec/

For information on accredited schools, teacher certification, financial aid, and careers in special education, contact:

National Clearinghouse for Professions in Special Education
1110 North Glebe Road, Suite 300
Arlington, VA 22201-5704
Tel: 800-641-7824
Email: ncpse@cec.sped.org
Web: http://www.special-ed-careers.org

Teacher Aides

School Subjects	Art English
Personal Skills	Helping/teaching Leadership/management
Work Environment	Primarily indoors Primarily one location
Minimum Education Level	High school diploma
Salary Range	$10,070 to $15,829 to $23,442+
Certification or Licensing	None available
Outlook	Faster than the average

Overview

Teacher aides perform a wide variety of duties to help teachers run a classroom. Teacher aides prepare instructional materials, help students with classroom work, and supervise students in the library, on the playground, and at lunch. They perform administrative duties such as photocopying, keeping attendance records, and grading papers. There are approximately 1.2 million teacher aides employed in the United States.

History

As formal education became more widely available in the 20th century, teachers' jobs became more complex. The size of classes increased, and a growing educational bureaucracy demanded that more records be kept of students' achievements and classroom activities. Advancements in technology, changes in educational theory, and a great increase in the amount and variety of teaching materials available all contributed to the time required to prepare materials and assess student progress, leaving teachers less time for the teaching for which they had been trained.

To remedy this problem, teacher aides began to be employed to take care of the more routine aspects of running an instructional program. Today, many schools and school districts employ teacher aides, to the great benefit of hardworking teachers and students.

The Job

Teacher aides work in public, private, and parochial preschools and elementary and secondary schools. Their duties vary depending on the classroom teacher, school, and school district. Some teacher aides specialize in one subject and some work in a specific type of school setting. These settings include bilingual classrooms, gifted and talented programs, classes for learning disabled students and those with unique physical needs, and multiage classrooms. These aides conduct the same type of classroom work as other teacher aides, but may provide more individual assistance to students.

Fran Moker works as a teacher aide in a dropout prevention unit of a middle school. Her work involves enrolling students in the unit and explaining the program to parents. She maintains files on the students and attends to other administrative duties. "I work directly with the sixth, seventh, and eighth grade teachers," Moker says, "making all the copies, setting up conferences, and grading papers. I also cover their classes when necessary for short periods of time to give the teachers a break." She also works directly with students, tutoring and advising. "I listen to students when they have problems," she says. "We work with at-risk students, so it's necessary to be supportive. Many of our students come from broken homes and have parents with serious drug and alcohol problems. Consistent caring is a must."

No matter what kind of classroom they assist in, teacher aides will likely copy, compile, and hand out class materials, set up and operate audiovisual equipment, arrange field trips, and type or word process materials. They organize classroom files, including grade reports, attendance, and health records. They may also obtain library materials and order classroom supplies.

Teacher aides may be in charge of keeping order in classrooms, school cafeterias, libraries, hallways, and playgrounds. Often, they wait with preschool and elementary students coming to or leaving school and make sure all students are accounted for. When a class leaves its room for such subjects as art, music, physical education, or computer lab, teacher aides may go with the students to help the teachers of these other subjects.

Another responsibility of teacher aides is correcting and grading homework and tests, usually for objective assignments and tests that require specific answers. They use answer sheets to mark students' papers and examinations and keep records of students' scores. In some large schools, an aide may be called a *grading clerk* and be responsible only for scoring objective tests and computing and recording test scores. Often using an electronic grading machine or computer, the grading clerk totals errors found and computes the percentage of questions answered correctly. The worker then records this score and averages students' test scores to determine their grade for the course.

Under the teacher's supervision, teacher aides may work directly with students in the classroom. They listen to a group of young students read aloud or involve the class in a special project such as a science fair, art project, or drama production. With older students, teacher aides provide review or study sessions prior to exams or give extra help with research projects or homework. Some teacher aides work with individual students in a tutorial setting, helping in areas of special need or concern. They may work with the teacher to prepare lesson plans, bibliographies, charts, or maps. They may help to decorate the classroom, design bulletin boards and displays, and arrange workstations. Teacher aides may even participate in parent-teacher conferences to discuss students' progress.

Requirements

High School

Courses in English, history, social studies, mathematics, art, drama, physical education, and the sciences will provide you with a broad base of knowledge. This knowledge will enable you to help students learn in these same subjects. Knowledge of a second language can be an asset, especially when working in schools with bilingual student, parent, or staff populations. Courses in child care, home economics, and psychology are also valuable for this career. You should try to gain some experience working with computers; students at many elementary schools and even preschools now do a large amount of computer work, and computer skills are important in performing clerical duties.

Postsecondary Training

Postsecondary requirements for teacher aides depend on the school or school district and the kinds of responsibilities the aides have. In districts where aides perform mostly clerical duties, applicants may need only to have a high school diploma or the equivalent, Graduation Equivalency Degree (GED). Those who work in the classroom may be required to take some college courses and attend in-service training and special teacher conferences and seminars. Some schools and districts help teacher aides pay some of the costs involved in attending these programs. Often community and junior colleges have certificate and associate's programs that prepare teacher aides for class-room work, offering courses in child development, health and safety, and child guidance.

Newly hired aides participate in orientation sessions and formal training at the school. In these sessions, aides learn about the school's organization, operation, and philosophy. They learn how to keep school records, operate audiovisual equipment, check books out of the library, and administer first aid.

Many schools prefer to hire teacher aides who have some experience working with children; some schools prefer to hire workers who live within the school district. Some schools may require teacher aide applicants to pass written exams and health physicals. All teacher aides must be able to work effectively with both children and adults and should have good verbal and written communications skills.

Other Requirements

You must enjoy working with children and be able to handle their demands, problems, and questions with patience and fairness. You must be willing and able to follow instructions, but also should be able to take the initiative in projects. Flexibility, creativity, and a cheerful outlook are definite assets for anyone working with children. You should find out the specific job require-ments from the school, school district, or state department of education in the area where you would like to work. Requirements vary from school to school and state to state. It is important to remember that an aide who is qualified to work in one state, or even one school, may not be qualified to work in another.

Exploring

You can gain experience working with children by volunteering to help with religious education classes at your place of worship. You may volunteer to help with scouting troops or work as a counselor at a summer camp. You may have the opportunity to volunteer to help coach a children's athletic team or work with children in after-school programs at community centers. Babysitting is a common way to gain experience in working with children and to learn about the different stages of child development.

Employers

With the national shortage of teachers, aides can find work in just about any preschool, elementary, or secondary school in the country. Teacher aides also assist in special education programs and in group home settings. Aides work in both public and private schools.

Starting Out

Applicants can apply directly to schools and school districts for teacher aide positions. Many school districts and state departments of education maintain job listings, bulletin boards, and hotlines that list available job openings. Teacher aide jobs are often advertised in the classified section of the newspaper. Once hired, teacher aides spend the first months in special training and will receive a beginning wage. After six months or so, they have regular responsibilities and possibly a wage increase.

Advancement

Teacher aides usually advance only in terms of increases in salary or responsibility, which come with experience. Aides in some districts may receive time off to take college courses. Some teacher aides choose to pursue bachelor's degrees and fulfill the licensing requirements of the state or school to become teachers. "I will probably always remain in the education field," Fran Moker says, "maybe someday returning to school to get a degree in education."

Some aides, who find that they enjoy the administrative side of the job, may move into school or district office staff positions. Others choose to get more training and then work as resource teachers, tutors, guidance counselors, or reading, mathematics, or speech specialists. Some teacher aides go into school library work or become media specialists. While it is true that most of these jobs require additional training, the job of teacher aide is a good place to begin.

Earnings

Teacher aides are usually paid on an hourly basis and usually only during the nine or ten months of the school calendar. Salaries vary depending upon the school or district, region of the country, and the duties the aides perform. Some teacher aides may earn as little as minimum wage while others earn up to $11.27 an hour, according to the U.S. Department of Labor. Median average annual salaries for teacher aides were $7.61 an hour in 1998.

Benefits such as health insurance and vacation or sick leave may also depend upon the school or district as well as the number of hours a teacher aide works. Many schools employ teacher aides only part time and do not offer such benefits. Other teacher aides may receive the same health and pension benefits as the teachers in their school and be covered under collective bargaining agreements.

Work Environment

Teacher aides work in a well-lit, comfortable, wheelchair-accessible environment, although some older school buildings may be in disrepair with unpredictable heating or cooling systems. Most of their work will be indoors, but teacher aides will spend some time outside before and after school, and during recess and lunch hours, to watch over the students. They are often on their feet, monitoring the halls and lunch areas, and running errands for teachers. Although this work is not physically strenuous, working closely with children can be stressful and tiring.

Teacher aides find it rewarding to help students learn and develop. The pay, however, is not as rewarding. "As with all those in the entire education field," Fran Moker says, "we are grossly underpaid. But that's the only negative. I truly enjoy my job." Because of her commitment to her work, Moker is allowed certain benefits, such as time off when needed.

Outlook

Growth in this field is expected to be much faster than the average into the next century because of an expected increase in the number of school-age children. The U.S. Department of Labor predicts that this field will grow by 31 percent, or 375,000 jobs, from 1998 to 2008. As the number of students in schools increases, new schools and classrooms will be added and more teachers and teacher aides will be hired. A shortage of teachers will find administrators hiring more aides to help with larger classrooms. Because of increased responsibilities for aides, state departments of education will likely establish standards of training. The National Resource Center for Paraprofessionals in Education and Related Services is designing national standards for paraeducator training.

The field of special education, that is, working with students with specific learning, emotional, or physical concerns or disabilities, is expected to grow rapidly, and more aides will be needed in these areas. The 1997 Individuals with Disabilities Education Act requires more specialized training for aides working with students with disabilities. Teacher aides who want to work with young children in day care or extended day programs will have a relatively easy time finding work because more children are attending these programs while their parents are at work.

For More Information

To learn about current education issues affecting aides, contact:

American Federation of Teachers
555 New Jersey Avenue, NW
Washington, DC 20001
Tel: 202-879-4400
Email: online@aft.org
Web: http://www.aft.org

To order publications or read current research and other information, contact:

Association for Childhood Education International
17904 Georgia Avenue, Suite 215
Olney, MD 20832
Tel: 301-570-2111
Email: aceihq@aol.com
Web: http://www.udel.edu/bateman/acei/

For information about training programs and other resources, contact:

National Resource Center for Paraprofessionals in Education and Related Services
Utah State University
6526 Old Main Hill
Logan, UT 84322-6526
Tel: 435-797-7272
Email: info@nrcpara.org
Web: http://www.nrcpara.org/

Tour Guides

Foreign language History	School Subjects
Helping/teaching Leadership/management	Personal Skills
Indoors and outdoors Primarily multiple locations	Work Environment
Some postsecondary training	Minimum Education Level
$9.75 to $20 to $30 per hour	Salary Range
Recommended	Certification or Licensing
Faster than the average	Outlook

Overview

Tour guides plan and oversee travel arrangements and accommodations for groups of tourists. They assist travelers with questions or problems, and may provide travelers with itineraries of their proposed travel route and plans. Tour guides research their destinations thoroughly so that they can handle any unforeseen situation that may occur.

History

People have always had a certain fascination with the unknown. Curiosity about distant cities and foreign cultures was one of the main forces behind the spread of civilization. Traveling in the ancient world was an arduous and sometimes dangerous task. Today, however, travel is commonplace. People travel for business, recreation, and education. School children may take field trips to their state's capitol, and some college students now have the opportunity to study in foreign countries. Recreation and vacation travel account for much of people's spending of their disposable income.

Early travelers were often accompanied by guides who had become familiar with the routes on earlier trips. When leisure travel became more commonplace in the 19th century, women and young children were not expected to travel alone, so relatives or house servants often acted as companions. Today, tour guides act as escorts for people visiting foreign countries and provide them with additional information on interesting facets of life in another part of the world. In a way, tour guides have taken the place of the early scouts, acting as experts in settings and situations that other people find unfamiliar.

The Job

Acting as knowledgeable companions and chaperons, tour guides escort groups of tourists to different cities and countries. Their job is to make sure that the passengers in a group tour enjoy an interesting and safe trip. To do this, they have to know a great deal about their travel destination and about the interests, knowledge, and expectations of the people on the tour.

One basic responsibility of tour guides is handling all the details of a trip prior to departure. They may schedule airline flights, bus trips, or train trips, as well as book cruises, house boats, or car rentals. They also research area hotels and other lodgings for the group and make reservations in advance. If anyone in the group has unique requirements, such as a specialized diet or a need for wheelchair accessibility, the tour guide will work to meet these requests.

Tour guides plan itineraries and daily activities, keeping in mind the interests of the group. For example, a group of music lovers visiting Vienna may wish to see the many sites of musical history there, as well as attend a performance by that city's orchestra. In addition to sight-seeing tours, guides may make arrangements in advance for special exhibits, dining experiences, and side trips. Alternate outings are sometimes planned in case of inclement weather conditions.

The second major responsibility of tour guides is, of course, the tour itself. Here, they must make sure all aspects of transportation, lodging, and recreation meet the itinerary as it was planned. They must see to it that travelers' baggage and personal effects are loaded and handled properly. If the tour includes meals and trips to local establishments, the guide must make sure that each passenger is on time for the various arrivals and departures.

Tour guides provide the people in their groups with interesting information on the locale and alert them to special sights. Tour guides become familiar with the history and significance of places through research and previous visits and endeavor to make the visit as entertaining and informative as possible. They may speak the native language or hire an interpreter in order to get along well with the local people. They are also familiar with local customs so their group will not offend anyone unknowingly. They see that the group stays together so that they do not miss their transportation arrangements or get lost. Guides may also arrange free time for travelers to pursue their individual interests, although time frames and common meeting points for regrouping are established in advance.

Even with thorough preparation, unexpected occurrences can arise on any trip and threaten to ruin everyone's good time. Tour guides must be resourceful to handle these surprises, such as when points of interest are closed or accommodations turn out to be unacceptable. They must be familiar with an area's resources so that they can help in emergencies such as an ill passenger or lost personal items. Tour guides often intercede on their travelers' behalf when any questions or problems arise regarding currency, restaurants, customs, or necessary identification.

Requirements

High School

Although tour guides do not need a college education, they should at least have a high school diploma. Courses such as speech, communications, art, sociology, anthropology, political science, and literature often prove beneficial. Some tour guides study foreign languages and cultures, as well as geography, history, and architecture.

Postsecondary Training

Some cities have professional schools that offer curricula in the travel industry. Such training may take nine to 12 months and offer job placement services. Some two- and four-year colleges offer tour guide training that lasts from six to eight weeks. Community colleges may offer programs in tour escort training. Programs such as these often may be taken on a part-time basis. Classes may include world geography, psychology, human relations, and communication courses. Sometimes students go on field trips themselves to gain experience. Some travel agencies and tour companies offer their own training so that their tour guides may receive instruction that complements the tour packages the company offers.

Certification or Licensing

The National Tour Association offers the Certified Tour Professional designation to candidates who complete 200 education credits in two areas: Professional Study and Professional Activity. Candidates must also have a minimum of five years of employment in the travel industry, unless they have a industry-specific degree from an accredited college or university. Candidates with a college degree must have a minimum of three years of industry employment.

Other Requirements

Tour guides are outgoing, friendly, and confident people. They are aware of the typical travelers' needs and the kinds of questions and concerns they might have. Tour guides are comfortable being in charge of large groups of people and have good time-management skills. They need to be resourceful and able to adapt to different environments. They are also fun-loving and know how to make others feel at ease in unfamiliar surroundings. Tour guides should enjoy working with people as much as they enjoy traveling.

Exploring

One way to become more familiar with the responsibilities of this job is to accompany local tours. Many cities have their own historical societies and museums that offer tours, as well as opportunities to volunteer. To appreciate what is involved with speaking in front of groups and the kind of research that may be necessary for leading tours, students may prepare speeches or presentations for class or local community groups.

Employers

The major employers of tour guides are, naturally, tour companies. Many tour guides work on a freelance basis, while others may own their own tour businesses.

Starting Out

Those interested in a career as a tour guide may begin as a guide for a museum or state park. This would be a good introduction to handling groups of people, giving lectures on points of interest or exhibits, and developing confidence and leadership qualities. Zoos, theme parks, historical sites, or local walking tours often need volunteers or part-time employees to work in their information centers, offer visitors directions, and answer a variety of inquiries. When openings occur, it is common for part-time workers to move into full-time positions.

Travel agencies, tour bus companies, and park districts often need additional help during the summer months when the travel season is in full swing. Societies and organizations for architecture and natural history, as well as other cultural groups, often train and employ guides. Students interested in working as tour guides for these types of groups should submit applications directly to the directors of personnel or managing directors.

Advancement

Tour guides gain experience by handling more complicated trips. Some workers may advance through specialization, such as tours to specific countries or to multiple destinations. Some tour guides choose to open their own travel agencies or work for wholesale tour companies, selling trip packages to individuals or retail tour companies.

Some tour guides become *travel writers* and report on exotic destinations for magazines and newspapers. Other guides may decide to work in the corporate world and plan travel arrangements for company executives. With the further development of the global economy, many different jobs have become available for people who know foreign languages and cultures.

Earnings

Tour guides may find that they have peak and slack periods of the year that correspond to vacation and travel seasons. Many tour guides, however, work eight months of the year. Salaries range from $9.75 to $20 an hour. Experienced guides with managerial responsibilities can earn up to $65,000 a year, including gratuities. According to *U.S. News & World Report,* the average salary for an entry-level inbound tour guide (tour guides who guide foreign visitors through famous American tourist sites) is $20,000, with average mid-level earnings approximately $35,000 per year. The most experienced guides can earn as much as $75,000 annually.

Guides receive their meals and accommodations free while conducting a tour, as well as a daily stipend to cover their personal expenses. Salaries and benefits vary, depending upon the tour operators that employ guides and the location they are employed in. Generally, the Great Lakes, Mid-Atlantic, Southeast, and Southern regions of the United States offer the highest compensation.

Tour guides very often receive paid vacations as part of their fringe benefits package; some may also receive sick pay and health insurance as well. Some companies may offer profit sharing and bonuses. They often receive discounts from hotels, airlines, and transportation companies in appreciation for repeat business.

Work Environment

The key word in the tour guide profession is variety. Most tour guides work in offices while they make travel arrangements and handle general business, but once on the road, they experience a wide range of accommodations, conditions, and situations. Tours to distant cities involve maneuvering through busy and confusing airports. Side trips may involve bus rides, train transfers, or private car rentals, all with varying degrees of comfort and reliability. Package trips that encompass seeing a number of foreign countries may require the guide to speak a different language in each city.

The constant feeling of being on the go, plus the responsibility of leading a large group of people, can sometimes be stressful. Unexpected events and uncooperative people have the capacity to ruin part of a trip for everyone involved, including the guide. However, the thrill of travel, discovery, and meeting new people can be so rewarding that all the negatives can be forgotten (or eliminated by preplanning on the next trip).

Outlook

Because of the many different travel opportunities for business, recreation, and education, there will be a significant need for tour guides through 2008. This demand is due in part to the fact that when the economy is strong, people earn more and are able to spend more on travel.

Tours for special interests, such as to ecologically significant areas and wilderness destinations, continue to grow in popularity. Although certain seasons are more popular for travel than others, well-trained tour guides can keep busy all year long.

Another area of tourism that is on the upswing is inbound tourism. Many foreign travelers view the United States as a dream destination, with tourist spots such as Disney World and Yellowstone National Park drawing millions of foreign visitors each year. Job opportunities in inbound tourism will likely be more plentiful than those guiding Americans in foreign locations. The best opportunities in inbound tourism are in large cities with international airports and in areas with a large amount of tourist traffic. Opportunities will also be better for those guides who speak foreign languages.

Aspiring tour guides should keep in mind that this field is highly competitive. Tour guide jobs, because of the obvious benefits, are highly sought after, and the beginning job seeker may find it difficult to break into the business. It is also important to remember that the travel and tourism industry is affected by the overall economy. When the economy is depressed, people have less money to spend and, therefore, travel less.

For More Information

For information on the travel industry and the related career of travel agent, contact:

American Society of Travel Agents
1101 King Street, Suite 200
Alexandria, VA 22314
Tel: 703-739-2782
Web: http://www.astanet.com

For information on internships, scholarships, the Certified Tour Professional designation, and a list of colleges and universities that offer tourism-related programs, contact:

National Tour Association
546 East Main Street
PO Box 3071
Lexington, KY 40508-2300
Tel: 800-682-8886
Web: http://www.ntaonline.com

Index

WS   SEP 0 5 2002